180
PRAYERS
FOR A
Woman of
Courage

180 PRAYERS
FOR A
Woman of Courage

SHANNA D. GREGOR

BARBOUR
PUBLISHING

Introduction

"This is my command—be strong and courageous! Do not be afraid or discouraged. For the LORD your God is with you wherever you go" (Joshua 1:9 NLT). Truly powerful, God-given courage is within your grasp. These 180 powerful prayers will align your heart and mind to live fearlessly, to stand confident and courageous in God's unending love and grace in every aspect of your life.

Your life of faith began with prayer and will continue throughout eternity as a constant exchange with the one who loves you most and knows you best. He desires a relationship with you, and your prayer time is an open invitation to know and experience Him.

Maybe you desire to talk to God regularly, but you struggle to know what to say. Perhaps you'd like to have more scripture to support your prayers and time with God. *180 Prayers for a Woman of Courage* is a collection of short, powerful prayers to get your conversation started with your heavenly Father, and each prayer includes a verse of scripture to inspire and encourage you.

Let these prayers motivate you to come boldly before your heavenly Father and spend time with Him. May these heartfelt words to God build your confidence as a woman of faith and infuse you with courage every day.

1

Console Me with Your Word

Help me, Lord, to capture my what-if thoughts and rein them in. I feel the worry rising, stirring my emotions. Before anxiety overwhelms me, console me with Your Word. When I worry about many things, Your assuring words soothe my soul. Remind me of the many promises You've made. You replace any fear with Your power, love, and sound thinking. When my heart becomes unsettled, Your gentle whispers anchor my soul. I am comforted in Your promise to never leave me or forsake me. I trust You always to go with me; I am never alone.

- - - - - - - - - - - - - -

When I worried about many things, your assuring words soothed my soul.
PSALM 94:19 GW

2

Seasons of Life

Jesus, You said this world is not without trouble. I am not exempt from the highs and lows, the mountains and valleys, so I will walk by faith and not by my feelings. May I always be thankful for all the seasons in life. May I praise You and rejoice when things are going well but even more so when there's difficulty and pain. Help me keep my focus on You, Lord. When the winter becomes unbearable or the summers of life grow uncomfortably hot, I will remember that nothing lasts forever. You are leading me, even when I cannot see what's next. By faith, I will follow You.

Everything is appropriate in its own time. But though God has planted eternity in the hearts of men, even so, many cannot see the whole scope of God's work from beginning to end.

ECCLESIASTES 3:11 TLB

3

My Deliverance

You are my deliverer. The heavy weight of life's challenges brings me to my knees, at the throne of Your grace. Thoughts of defeat overwhelm me, and yet I remember the Israelites standing between the Egyptians and the Red Sea. Their oppressors were closing in fast, and fear of returning to captivity pressed in. Miraculously You parted the sea and made a way of escape for them. You will do the same for me. Nothing is impossible for You. You will show me the way out in Your time. I trust that my deliverance is on its way.

Moses spoke to the people: "Don't be afraid. Stand firm and watch God do his work of salvation for you today. Take a good look at the Egyptians today for you're never going to see them again."
EXODUS 14:13 MSG

4

In the Waiting

Waiting is hard for me. I want a swift resolution to this hardship, but it hasn't come yet. I need Your help while waiting. Repeatedly, I set my eyes on the finish line only to lose my focus. I'm stuck in the muck of difficulty. Even though I'm trudging along at a snail's pace and I can't see what You're doing, Lord, I refuse to stop. I won't give up. I trust You. I will wait. I will look up and see my salvation that can only come from You. I hold tightly to You today.

- - - - - - - - - - - - - - - - - - - -

I waited patiently for the LORD. He turned to me and heard my cry for help. He pulled me out of a horrible pit, out of the mud and clay. He set my feet on a rock and made my steps secure.
PSALM 40:1–2 GW

5

One Voice to Follow

Lord, You are my Good Shepherd. Help me tune my ears to Your voice. I refuse to follow anyone's direction but Yours. As I fellowship with You in Your Word and in prayer, I know You more and more. I hear You in the quiet times. I listen for instruction, especially when danger approaches. When I am distracted or tempted to wander away on my own, call me back to You. Speak to me and comfort me. Correct me so that I won't miss a step on the path You've chosen for me. Yours is the only voice I need to hear. May all other voices grow dull.

"My sheep recognize my voice, and I know them, and they follow me. I give them eternal life and they shall never perish."
John 10:27–28 TLB

6

Christ Jesus My Intercessor

Jesus, You went to the cross, spent time in hell, and rose from the grave in order to bring me back into relationship with the Father. You did not come to condemn me but to give me eternal life. When Satan condemns me or accuses me, remind me that You are my Advocate. You go before me interceding for me. You make a way when there seems to be no way. You understand when no one else does. You bring me up from the messes I find myself in. You are always on my side, giving me hope and a reason to press on.

- - - - - - - - - - - - - - - - - - - -

Who is he who condemns? It is Christ
who died, and furthermore is also risen,
who is even at the right hand of God,
who also makes intercession for us.
ROMANS 8:34 NKJV

7

Unshakable

When the earth moves beneath me because of the circumstances of my life, I look to You, Lord. When hope threatens to escape me, You are the one I hold on to. You are my stability and strength. My heart will remain steady despite all I see. I turn my eyes to You. I look up because You are my light and my salvation. When opposition raises its head against me, I refuse to fear. It cannot hold me within its prison bars. I remain free and unshakable because You hold me in the palm of Your hand.

- -

My heart will not be afraid even if an army rises to attack. I know that you are there for me, so I will not be shaken.
PSALM 27:3 TPT

8

Always with Me

Fear comes like a dark shadow to engulf me, but I refuse to become fear's prisoner. As the waves of doubt and unbelief try to wash me away, I remind myself that You are always with me. You are my hope, my light, my salvation. You shine Your life into my situation. You bring peace into my heart and settle me. You speak courage and I draw strength from Your words. I am comforted by Your presence, and the storm around me roars no more. Fill me with Your peace now.

- - - - - - - - - - - - - - - -

Immediately he spoke to them and said, "Take courage! It is I. Don't be afraid." Then he climbed into the boat with them, and the wind died down. They were completely amazed.
MARK 6:50–51 NIV

9

The Way of Escape

I call on You today, my Redeemer, my Rock. I can depend on You to always do what You have promised. You are always there to help when I call. Give me wisdom to navigate the path before me. Keep me on the right path, and alert me to the traps ahead. Help me avoid the snares of the enemy. Give me strength to endure the difficulty I'm facing, knowing that You have provided a way of escape. Open my eyes to see the path You've chosen. I listen for Your instruction now.

God, who faithfully keeps his promises,
will not allow you to be tempted beyond your
power to resist. But when you are tempted,
he will also give you the ability to endure
the temptation as your way of escape.
1 Corinthians 10:13 gw

10

Boldness to Go

Heavenly Father, You have great plans for me, and I don't want to miss one single thing. Today I set my heart in alignment with Your will. I will obediently answer Your call and willingly do what You ask. Bring people across my path who will join with me in Your purposes, and help me know who they are. Give me boldness to do whatever You ask. I am determined to stay focused on You. I will not be deterred. Prepare me for the things ahead. Direct my path, and help me move forward when You say, "Go!" Clear the path before me.

Paul. . .welcomed all who visited him, telling them with all boldness about the Kingdom of God and about the Lord Jesus Christ; and no one tried to stop him.
Acts 28:30–31 TLB

11

Never Anxious

When I'm tempted to allow my thoughts to pull me under the waters of anxiety, remind me that You never want me to be anxious about anything. I don't need to be worried. Today I spend time saturating my soul in prayer. Help me offer up faith-filled requests to You throughout the day. I will overflow with gratitude and thanksgiving. Thank You that I can share every detail of my life with You, knowing I won't be condemned or judged but comforted. Thank You for Your wonderful peace that surpasses my own human understanding. Thank You for an immediate inner calm in my heart. When my soul is anxious, I will hold tightly to Your promise of peace.

Be anxious for nothing, but in everything by prayer and supplication, with thanksgiving, let your requests be made known to God.
PHILIPPIANS 4:6 NKJV

12

The Answer Is on the Way

Lord, You know my prayer requests before they ever cross my lips, and yet, I know You desire for me to ask. So today, I am asking You to perfect those things that weigh heavily on my heart and mind. I trust that You have already started working behind the scenes on my behalf. You know the details and how they should work out best for me. The answer I need, whether I know it's what I need or not, is on its way. Help me patiently wait for Your perfect work to be perfected in my situation.

"The moment you began praying a command was given. I am here to tell you what it was, for God loves you very much. Listen and try to understand the meaning of the vision that you saw!"
DANIEL 9:23 TLB

13

Lord, Help!

It's the simplest prayer, Lord, and I don't say it nearly enough. I was created to need Your assistance. I should always look to You to provide the answers I need, but sometimes I don't. Forgive me when I look to others for the answers You alone can provide. Remind me that the solution is always in my best interest when I ask You. You always wait patiently for me to ask. I know I'm sometimes slow in doing so. Help me not to lean on my own understanding or try to work things out on my own, but to always reach out to You. You have promised, and today I'm asking for Your help.

- - - - - - - - - - - - - -

"For I am the Lord your God who takes hold of your right hand and says to you, Do not fear; I will help you."
ISAIAH 41:13 NIV

14

I Can Never Be Forgotten

Praise You, God! You will never abandon me. You cannot forget me! No matter how I feel or what crazy thoughts run through my head, I belong to You. I refuse to be moved by my emotions because they always fail me. I am Your covenant child. I hold tightly to that truth. You will never forsake me. When I feel lost or alone, I imagine Your hand with who I am to You engraved deeply into Your palm. You will never lose sight of me. I remain constantly on Your mind and in Your view. My relationship with You is the reality. I am holding tightly to Your promises, believing Your truth.

---

*I have engraved you on the palms of my hands.
Your walls are always in my presence.*
ISAIAH 49:16 GW

15

I Will Not Drown

When the weight of difficult circumstances crashes in on me, I am tempted to let it take me down. Then I remember Your promise to always be with me. No matter how high the waters get, no matter how much I feel like I will drown, You hold me up. You are my flotation device. You have promised not to let the waters overtake me. I will rise above the waters by Your holy hand. I depend on You to carry me through the rough waters. I will trust You to help me navigate the safest passage. I hold tightly to You, my salvation, and I will praise You now and always.

When you go through deep waters and great trouble, I will be with you. When you go through rivers of difficulty, you will not drown!
ISAIAH 43:2 TLB

16

A Well-Founded Hope

In the middle of a discouraging diagnosis, Your encouragement prevails. I believe You can and will heal, but I am struggling along the way. Console and encourage me during this difficulty. Give me hope when I feel hopeless. Bring others across my path to remind me of Your love and mercy. I place great hope and earnest expectation in You. May I stand steadfast in the face of adversity, trusting You every step of the way to overcome this season in my life.

Now may our Lord Jesus Christ Himself and God our Father, Who loved us and gave us everlasting consolation and encouragement and well-founded hope through [His] grace (unmerited favor), comfort and encourage your hearts and strengthen them [make them steadfast and keep them unswerving] in every good work and word.
2 THESSALONIANS 2:16–17 AMPC

17

Cheers to Giving

God, You are a generous giver. Your Word says You will provide seed to the sower and in due season I will reap a harvest. Thank You for the seed I've sown and for the harvest that is on the way. I realize what I have to give goes far beyond financial gifts. Open my eyes to any opportunity You set before me to give cheerfully. I appreciate each opportunity to be generous. Show me the many different ways You would have me give into the lives of others. Just as You meet all my needs, may I remain openhanded, ready to help others in every way I can.

- - - - - - - - - - - - - -

Each of you should give whatever you have decided. You shouldn't be sorry that you gave or feel forced to give, since God loves a cheerful giver.
2 Corinthians 9:7 GW

18

Placing the Puzzle Pieces

With strong assurance I know that You are my partner in this plan You have for me. Thank You for Your promise that all things work together for my good. Your plan is like a big puzzle, but I don't have a picture of what that puzzle looks like when it's finished. So as I put the pieces together, lead me through the work. I trust You to put the pieces in the right places so that when it is finished, my life looks exactly the way You have envisioned it. I hold tightly to Your hand and follow Your specific direction today.

- - - - - - - - - - - - - - - -

We are assured and know that [God being a partner in their labor] all things work together and are [fitting into a plan] for good to and for those who love God and are called according to [His] design and purpose.

ROMANS 8:28 AMPC

19

True Joy

I know that every person has individual battles. Many silently suffer through tough circumstances. May my life exude true joy from You. I don't want to pretend or deny what I'm going through, but not everyone needs to know what's going on with me. Help me share Your joy with others, bringing positivity and encouragement. Thank You for those close friends that I trust to share my struggles with. Remind me to also lend a hand and give support to them in their time of need. I want to be a heart with ears so that I can help them navigate life with joy. May I bring healing to those around me, always.

A cheerful heart does good like medicine,
but a broken spirit makes one sick.
PROVERBS 17:22 TLB

20

Faith Always Produces

God, I look back at where I've been as I'm facing another trial, and I see that You've been faithful. As I trust You now, I know that You have a plan. You always bring me through. Help me not to grow tired. Honestly, sometimes I do want to give up. But then where would I be? I'd be stuck. I cannot quit. I must press on. You are my hope. You will deliver me from this hardship. I will eventually come out on the other side, as long as I hold on to You. My faith in You always produces Your very best for me because You love me and You will never fail me.

- - - - - - - - - - - - - - - - - - - -

Consider it pure joy, my brothers and sisters, whenever you face trials of many kinds, because you know that the testing of your faith produces perseverance.
JAMES 1:2–3 NIV

21

Let My Life Shine

Heavenly Father, I want to let my light—the life that comes from You—shine before everyone. Create in me a clean heart, and cleanse me from all selfishness. My life will only shine if You are the source. I don't want to just get by, living a casual Christian life. I want my life to make a difference. Teach me to live and act in a way that speaks Your truth to others. Fill me with an undying passion to see lives changed for Your glory. When I'm called to defend my faith, help me do it in love, with gentleness and respect.

Light exposes the true character of everything because light makes everything easy to see. That's why it says: "Wake up, sleeper! Rise from the dead, and Christ will shine on you."
EPHESIANS 5:13–14 GW

22

I Believe

Thank You for the stories in Your Word about people who struggled to believe. At times I struggle to believe. In my heart of hearts, I know You will deliver on Your promises. You never fail me, God. You are not a man; You cannot lie. But the weight of my troubles puts pressure on my soul. I fight the negative thoughts in my mind. I know I need to let go and not think about them, but continually I have to take those thoughts captive and replace them with Your Word. I need Your help! I will fill my heart with Your promises by reading Your promises. Help my unbelief.

- - - - - - - - - - - - -

Jesus said to him, "If you can believe, all things are possible to him who believes." Immediately the father of the child cried out and said with tears, "Lord, I believe; help my unbelief!"
MARK 9:23–24 NKJV

23

Knowing Where to Draw the Line

Lord, I know it's easier to resist temptation if I've formed my convictions long before the temptation arrives. I resolve to be devoted to You and Your Word. This world I live in is full of compromise—it's expected, even from Christians. Help me know what I believe and what is acceptable in Your sight. Give me wisdom to think through my response to the temptations that may come. Help me know where to draw the line, and help me stay committed to not crossing those lines. Give me strength in my own convictions because of my love for You.

But Daniel determined that he would not defile himself by eating the king's food or drinking his wine, so he asked the head of the palace staff to exempt him from the royal diet.
DANIEL 1:8 MSG

24

Living in the Now

Lord, sometimes I feel like I'm living in a strange land, helpless and hopeless because of my anxiety about the future. I give You permission to be sovereign over my past, present, and future. I want to live in the moment. I regret spending time wondering about future events and waiting for certain things to happen so I can be happy. I trust You to work out the details. I will not worry about how You're going to do it but just trust that You will. I put my thoughts on You and Your promises. I choose to live in the now, this moment called today.

---

*"Be strong and courageous. Do not
be afraid or terrified because of them,
for the L*ORD *your God goes with you;
he will never leave you nor forsake you."*
DEUTERONOMY **31:6** NIV

25

For Loved Ones to Know

Jesus, it's difficult serving You when those I love most don't know You. I can't seem to make them understand. I want them to have a better life and assurance of eternal life in You. I don't want to argue or defend my relationship with You. Holy Spirit, lead me so that I know when to speak and when to be quiet. Help me choose words and actions that let them see You in me. I pray they see the difference You've made in my own life and will come to know You too. Bring someone into their lives that they will listen to, if it's not me.

Oh, the joys of those who do not follow evil men's advice, who do not hang around with sinners, scoffing at the things of God.
PSALM 1:1 TLB

26

Belong to the God of the Living

Lord, You created me. You know my history and my future. You placed me on this earth to live a life pleasing to You, to know You and to serve You. No one else knows me like You do. I am grateful to be a part of Your family. I am thankful for all You've done in my life. I never have to wonder where I belong. I belong to You. You guide and direct me. Help me hear Your voice. Help me to always be in the right place at the right time to do Your will.

- -

"Don't you realize that God was speaking directly to you when he said, 'I am the God of Abraham, Isaac, and Jacob'? So God is not the God of the dead, but of the living."
MATTHEW 22:31–32 TLB

27

Staying Spiritually Fit

Heavenly Father, what I allow to go into my heart is important to You—and me. The things I think about make an impression on my soul. What I hear and see produces thoughts that lead to actions. Help me not to deceive myself by thinking I can rise above the negative input. I will be courageous and refuse to partake of things that I shouldn't. As I spend time in the Bible, thinking about who You are and what Your Word means, it fuels my faith. Help me stay faithful to growing in Your Word. Give me a deep desire to stay spiritually fit.

"Don't for a minute let this Book of The Revelation be out of mind. Ponder and meditate on it day and night, making sure you practice everything written in it. Then you'll get where you're going; then you'll succeed."

JOSHUA 1:8 MSG

28

A Good Mother

Children are important to You. And I am thankful for the children You've given me—my own children as well as all other children in my life. I want to be the mother You created me to be. When thoughts of self-doubt sink into my mind, remind me that I can do all things through You. The Holy Spirit gives me wisdom to respond to their needs. Your love has been poured into my heart to show grace and mercy, especially when my emotions are shot. Each day, by faith, I believe You will help me be the mother my children need.

- - - - - - - - - - - - -

He put a child in the middle of the room.
Then, cradling the little one in his arms,
he said, "Whoever embraces one of these
children as I do embraces me, and far
more than me—God who sent me."
MARK 9:36–37 MSG

29

Great Faith

Why is it so hard to trust You sometimes? You have never failed me, and yet I struggle. I want to be full of faith. I want to accept every promise You make and believe they will happen for me, but sometimes I fear. Help me trust You. Help me have great faith. Today, I let go of my doubt. I surrender fully to You. Whatever is before me, I am determined to trust Your Word. You will not fail me. I can always count on You. You have said it, and I believe it. Help me continue to grow in faith.

Jesus marveled at this. He turned around and said to the crowd who had followed him, "Listen, everyone! Never have I found even one among the people of God a man like this who believes so strongly in me."
LUKE 7:9 TPT

30

Throwing off the Weight

I refuse to be a prisoner of anxiety. You have freed me from the grave. You are my Healer and my Redeemer. Help me focus on what is good and lovely—the things that come from You. Worry is my enemy, trying to steal my life and my health. But You are my joy. You are my strength. With Your help, I can throw off the weight of anxiety with courage and inspiration from Your Word. Bring relationships into my life that lift me up. Give me friends and family that make me laugh and remind me of Your goodness. Bring positive and encouraging words into my day. Thank You for praise and worship music that brings light and life to me.

- - - - - - - - - - - - - - - - - -

A person's anxiety will weigh him down,
but an encouraging word makes him joyful.
PROVERBS 12:25 GW

31

Holding on to His Promise

God, when You speak a word, it cannot return void. It always accomplishes what You send it to do. So when You make a promise, I believe it will definitely happen. The challenge is that time passes from when You give Your word to the end result. In that time I need to hold tightly to what You've said and not let doubt enter my mind or talk me out of what I believe You will do in my life. Help me stay strong and stand in faith. I will have courage! I trust that no matter how long it takes, it will be exactly as You've said. Your Word is forever true.

- -

"So have courage, men! I trust God that
everything will turn out as he told me."
ACTS 27:25 GW

32

Face-to-Face

I am created for relationship with You. Remind me daily that You desire face time with me. Just as You walked in the garden with Adam and talked with him, You desire that same fellowship with me. I will take time for You. I will not allow the busyness of life to overcrowd us. Help me know what You want me to be a part of, and teach me to say no to those things that I should not give my time to. I press into Your presence for an encounter with You now. Just as Moses asked to see Your glory (Exodus 33:18), I too want to see Your glory. Speak to me face-to-face.

- -

The Lord would speak to Moses face to face, as one speaks to a friend.
Exodus 33:11 niv

33

Committed to Your Word

I love Your Word. Your ways are always just and right. I take the path You have chosen for me because Your Word preserves my life. I will walk in the way Your Word compels me to go. Help me follow hard after You with all my heart. Help me keep my heart right so that I always do what pleases You most. When I am weary, help me keep Your commandments. When I am not sure which way to go, light my way with biblical truths. I am committed to Your Word, God. I take it to heart so that I will not sin against You. Help me hear Your voice directing my path!

- - - - - - - - - - - - - - - - - -

How I long for your precepts! In your
righteousness preserve my life.
PSALM 119:40 NIV

34

My Help Comes from the Lord

Heavenly Father, I come to You first. I will overcome this world, just as Jesus did, through prayer. Help me remember that I don't have to do this life alone. You are with me—helping me, guiding me, protecting me, and cheering me on. I receive strength from You. I listen to Your wisdom. As I spend time with You, I emerge confident and strong. I hold fast to You knowing the storms of life will not take me out. Whatever I need today, You will provide it. I refuse to lose. I will not give up. Keep me in all my ways as I acknowledge You today.

- - - - - - - - - - - - - - - - - - -

Shall I look to the mountain gods for help?
No! My help is from Jehovah who made
the mountains! And the heavens too!
PSALM 121:1–2 TLB

35

Pursue the New

Thank You for my new life. I am reborn in Christ, but sometimes I slip back into my old thought patterns, remembering who I was before. I know I should not beat myself up about my past. I am not that old person. I have a new life, new hopes, new dreams. As I study Your Word, help me renew my mind with the truth of who I am now and who You have created me to be. I intentionally put my past behind me. I focus on my future in You. Give me grace to forgive myself, to look past my failures, and to humbly pursue the new.

- -

*Anyone united with the Messiah gets
a fresh start, is created new. The old
life is gone; a new life emerges!*
2 CORINTHIANS 5:17 MSG

36

Divine Connections

Jesus, it's natural for me to be a little unsure about people I don't know. Even when I hear that they have a personal relationship with You, I am hesitant. Your Word says I can know others by the fruit produced in their lives. Still, I need Your wisdom and discernment for my relationships. Give me a calm assurance and peace for those divine connections You want in my life. Open my eyes to see others as You see them. Show me how to be a blessing in their lives.

So Ananias went over and found Paul and laid his hands on him and said, "Brother Paul, the Lord Jesus, who appeared to you on the road, has sent me so that you may be filled with the Holy Spirit and get your sight back."
ACTS 9:17 TLB

37

Say and Do Good

Lord, my words really matter. What I say about myself and about others is important. My words lead to actions, and my actions demonstrate the fruit growing in my life. I want to please You and produce good fruit for others to see—the kind of fruit that points them to You. Please place a guard over my mouth. Help me think about the words I say before I speak them. I want my words and actions to bring blessing and life into my life and into the lives of others. May I be an encourager who offers hope in all I say and do.

God our Father loved us and by his kindness gave us everlasting encouragement and good hope. Together with our Lord Jesus Christ, may he encourage and strengthen you to do and say everything that is good.
2 Thessalonians 2:16–17 gw

38

Help Me Hope Again

Lord, You make all things beautiful in their time. My life looks so different today than it did before I met You. I know You are working on me. Sometimes it's hard to escape the pain. Tears cloud my vision, and I struggle to find my way. But I know You are making me new. I won't give up hope, because Your promises are true. Even though I can't see it now, You have a plan to use me in wonderful ways. I give my all to You. Mold me, shape me. Help me hope again.

- - - - - - - - - - - - - - - - -

He has made everything beautiful in its time. Also He has put eternity in their hearts, except that no one can find out the work that God does from beginning to end.
ECCLESIASTES 3:11 NKJV

39

No One Loves Me Like You Do

Lord, You have always known everything there is to know about me. You realize every movement of my heart and soul, and You comprehend every thought before it ever enters my mind. My heart is Your open book, and You know all the words I'll say in a day before my feet hit the ground. You know every step I will take before my journey even begins. You've gone into my future to prepare my way. Thank You for Your hand of love on my life and for the blessings You impart to me. There is no one who loves me like You do.

- - - - - - - - - - - - - - -

You saw who you created me to be before I became me! Before I'd ever seen the light of day, the number of days you planned for me were already recorded in your book.
PSALM 139:16 TPT

40

Powerful Words

Father, Your Word is life to me. It brings me peace, security, joy, and understanding about who You are and who You've created me to be. Help me be a student of Your Word. I put Your Word in my heart so that it is with me when I need it most. I speak Your truth and it silences the words of doubt and fear that Satan whispers to bring worry and anxiety into my life. May Your life-giving words always triumph over any other voice I hear.

- - - - - - - - - - - - - - - - - - - -

Dear friend, listen well to my words; tune your ears to my voice. Keep my message in plain view at all times. Concentrate! Learn it by heart! Those who discover these words live, really live; body and soul, they're bursting with health.
PROVERBS 4:20–22 MSG

41

My Place in Prayer

Lord, I am a part of the household of faith. My connection to the family of God defines who I am. I am confident of my spiritual heritage and my eternal home in heaven. I am committed to prayer. It is the way I communicate with You. Through prayer our relationship grows. Through daily meditation I better understand myself and the heart of the Father. I grow in my trust and discover Your will and Your purposes. Thank You for my place in prayer. May I remain committed to my quiet moments with You. May our times together nurture my faith.

But Christ is a faithful son in charge of God's household. We are his household if we continue to have courage and to be proud of the confidence we have.
HEBREWS 3:6 GW

42

Exactly What Is Needed

Heavenly Father, You are the restorer of the breach. You bring healing to all the broken places in my life—not because I cry out to You, but because restoration is Your plan. You have a purpose. And even though I want the circumstances to change immediately, I wait for You with patience, with trust, and with faith because You will bring about what I need. It may not be what I want. It may not happen the way I think it will or the way I want it to. But it will be exactly what is needed. You know me better than I know myself, so I open my heart and ask You to do Your very best.

- - - - - - - - - - - - - - - -

"Behold, I will bring it health and healing;
I will heal them and reveal to them the
abundance of peace and truth."
JEREMIAH 33:6 NKJV

43

Unswerving Love

From the beginning of time, You had a plan for me. You loved me so much, You refused to lose. You sacrificed for the opportunity of a relationship with me. Oh, how great is Your unswerving love. You will never give up on me, no matter how many times I fail, no matter how many times I come to You asking for forgiveness. Thank You for Your great mercy. Thank You for guiding me with Your steady hand. May I always see Your love at every turn of the path You've set before me. I am no longer of this world but forever belong to You. May I live each day fully aware of Your sacrificial love for me.

- -

But God showed his great love for us by sending Christ to die for us while we were still sinners.
Romans 5:8 tlb

44

Overflowing Life

God, You are the giver of life. You hold my times in Your hands. But You've also enriched my life in ways I've never dreamed. You fill me to overflowing. Help me to always be watchful and aware of the enemy's plans. I will not be fearful of him but rely on You to keep me in all my ways. I am wise and have great understanding and discernment from You so that I stay on Your path. I will keep my eyes on You. I am laser focused. Thank You for every blessing. Even in the challenging times, You teach me Your ways and fill me with Your love.

The thief comes only in order to steal and kill and destroy. I came that they may have and enjoy life, and have it in abundance (to the full, till it overflows).
JOHN 10:10 AMPC

45

Restore, Heal, and Cure

God, You are my Creator. You know me from the inside out. When You created me, You made me individual and unique. Every challenge I've had with my health is no mystery to You. Doctors may treat an ailment, but You restore me, heal me, and cure me. You deliver me body, mind, and spirit. You know my emotional state and what things impact me positively and negatively. You will never give up on me. You will never fail me. Thank You for being there every single time I need You. Reach into me and bring about life-giving health as only You can.

- - - - - - - - - - - - - - - - -

"As for you, I'll come with healing, curing the incurable, because they all gave up on you and dismissed you as hopeless— that good-for-nothing Zion."
JEREMIAH 30:17 MSG

46

Teach Me to Pray

When I pray, I grow in faith. In Your presence my doubts and fears die. In Your presence my ability to trust You grows. Like Jesus, I want to be rooted in prayer. I want to walk in Your power and authority with signs and wonders. Just as Jesus taught His disciples to pray, I ask You, God, to teach me to pray. Help me to make prayer a priority, to esteem my time with You and guard it as a precious opportunity. May You find me daily on my knees before You, where I receive the strength and the courage I need to face the challenges of this fallen world.

- -

Once Jesus was praying in a certain place. When he stopped praying, one of his disciples said to him, "Lord, teach us to pray as John taught his disciples."
LUKE 11:1 GW

47

A Member of God's House

Lord, I am thankful for the Holy Spirit at work in my life. I gladly accept His help as I continue to grow in my faith. You have set a perfect example for me as a child of God. I pray that I can always strive to reflect You when others look at my life. I am grateful for Your faithfulness over Your house. May I always look to You first for answers for my life. I am confident in my faith and proud to belong to the household of faith.

- - - - - - - - - - - - - - - -

But Christ is a faithful son in charge of God's household. We are his household if we continue to have courage and to be proud of the confidence we have.
HEBREWS 3:6 GW

48

Daily Guidance

Forgive me, Father, for the times I've run to You only when life gets difficult. I know I should seek Your guidance by being in Your presence every day. Help me say no to distractions that would keep me from spending time with You. Fill me with an overwhelming desire to be with You. Help me continually seek You so that I am always prepared for any challenge of life. Through Your daily guidance I can better navigate the obstacles in life and in many cases avoid them. Draw me to You, God. May I hunger and thirst after You!

God, hear my cry. Show me your grace. Show me mercy, and send the help I need! Lord, when you said to me, "Seek my face," my inner being responded, "I'm seeking your face with all my heart."

PSALM 27:7–8 TPT

49

To See the Victory

Lord, sometimes it's hard to see the victory hidden in life's circumstances. As You hung on the cross, Your followers perceived it as a crushing defeat. They couldn't see what You could see. Even as You assured them, they couldn't see how Your death could bring victory. But once You rose again, they learned the eternal joy of having You with them always. Thank You for knowing the whole story. My victory is assured, and I will rejoice. I will see Your purpose and plan fulfilled in my life. You have made a way when I can't see it. So, I put my trust in You today. Help me rest in You.

- - - - - - - - - - - - - - -

"You have sorrow now, but I will see you
again and then you will rejoice; and
no one can rob you of that joy."
JOHN 16:22 TLB

50

His Power at Work

Thank You, Lord, for the opportunity to live for You. I recognize the Holy Spirit's power at work in my life today. Just as I trusted Jesus to begin my new life by faith, I choose to live each day trusting Him. Guide me in all I do, as I submit to Your will. I desire to live my life in the flow of Your blessing. I seek to learn more each day as I grow in understanding and wisdom.

In the same way you received Jesus our Lord and Messiah by faith, continue your journey of faith, progressing further into your union with him! Your spiritual roots go deeply into his life as you are continually infused with strength, encouraged in every way. For you are established in the faith you have absorbed and enriched by your devotion to him!
COLOSSIANS 2:6–7 TPT

51

For My Husband

Lord, help me be a support to my husband. Teach me to love him in every way that I should. Help me know how to encourage him emotionally and physically. I'll leave the spiritual needs to You. Let my words be a blessing to him. Give him favor with every person he meets, in his job, in his education, and in his friendships. Everything that he does, Lord, help him do it well as if he were doing it for You. Draw him closer to You, and help us live our lives together focused on You. Teach us to pray together and rely on You in the decisions we make as a couple.

- -

For I know the thoughts that I think toward you, says the LORD, thoughts of peace and not of evil, to give you a future and a hope.
JEREMIAH 29:11 NKJV

52

Continually Watchful

Lord, help me to actively wait for Your return just as the Corinthians waited for Paul's next visit. I will be on guard against spiritual enemies like sin, strife, pride, division, or false teachings—anything that might threaten my walk of faith. I will stand firm in what I believe, the truth that brought me salvation. I will be strong and courageous in the strength You've given me by Your Holy Spirit. I will embrace Your love and point others to the knowledge of who You are, because Your love is constantly at work in me. I do all things by Your love. Open my eyes to see what is often unseen. Reveal to me Your plans as I continue to watch and wait.

- - - - - - - - - - - - - - - - - - -

Be alert. Be firm in the Christian faith.
Be courageous and strong.
1 CORINTHIANS 16:13 GW

53

Less Drama, More Peace

Lord, I come to You today asking for peace in my family. Thank You for Your Spirit living in us and with us. My family is blessed when we come in and when we go out with Your peace. No matter how much chaos is going on around us, we can rest and rely on You. Help us not to lose our composure when chaos erupts. Remind us to fix our minds and hearts on You. The world is filled with drama, but it doesn't have to be a part of our life. Help us keep Your peace as the center of our home.

And all your [spiritual] children shall be disciples [taught by the Lord and obedient to His will], and great shall be the peace and undisturbed composure of your children.
ISAIAH 54:13 AMPC

54

Unexpected Gifts

God, I am grateful for the surprises You bring into my life, even when they catch me unawares and I'm not quite sure how to respond. Everything that comes from You is good, so I must remember to look at Your unexpected acts as gifts from You. Help me keep an open mind when new things appear in my life suddenly. Help me pause and stay calm when it's not something I planned. Remind me to ask if this is a part of Your plan. Give me patience as the gifts You send unfold. Sometimes it takes a little time to see and understand the purpose You have in mind.

"After all, he's famous for great and unexpected acts; there's no end to his surprises."
JOB 5:9 MSG

55

Speak the Word during Temptation

Jesus, You were tempted like any other man. You responded to temptation and the enemy with the Word of God after a time of prayer and fasting. You knew God's opinion on any situation You faced. Help me know God's desires for my life. Teach me to use Your Word during the battles I face, especially those occurring in my mind. When the devil tempts me, remind me of scripture. I will speak God's words in every part of my life. With the power of the Word and prayer, I can overcome temptation!

With my whole heart I have sought You; oh, let me not wander from Your commandments! Your word I have hidden in my heart, that I might not sin against You.
PSALM 119:10–11 NKJV

56

Words Are Life

I can only image what it was like when You spoke the world into existence. Your words created the earth and everything in it. The sound of Your voice has indescribable power. My Bible is full of Your words. Through Your Word I have come to know You. Each chapter and verse is filled with wisdom and understanding for my life. It is food for my spirit. Help me remember when I read my Bible that Your Word gives me life. Your Word sustains me. And when I pray according to Your Word, all of heaven is backing me up. I rejoice in Your Word. As I go about my day, bring Your Word alive in me. Remind me of Your truth.

- -

"Heaven and earth will pass away,
but my words will never pass away."
MATTHEW 24:35 NIV

57

Joyful, Always!

Heavenly Father, I can be an emotional person. But even while acknowledging what is going on around me, I can still maintain my trust in You. I can be unshakable if I have established my dependence on You alone. I refuse to allow my circumstances to make me waver. I will remain cheerful no matter what because my joy comes from You. I will maintain an attitude of prayer, ready to receive from You. And I will live my life in Christ, fully unmovable in my decision to do what You say. As I do Your will, help me embrace a joyful and thankful way of thinking, always.

Be cheerful no matter what; pray all the time; thank God no matter what happens. This is the way God wants you who belong to Christ Jesus to live.
1 THESSALONIANS 5:16–18 MSG

58

A Bold Faith

Because of what You've done, Jesus, my sins are forgiven and my transgressions are not counted against me. Through You, I am set apart. I have a hope and a future. I am considered righteous—but it's only through the glorious gift of God that I have a right standing with Him. And for this reason, I can live my life with confidence in You. I can stand solid in my faith, bold as a lion. Never let me take this precious gift for granted. Help me be brave, daring, and courageous even when people oppose Your truth. I will declare it and share it with others. Let my life be a testimony of Your great love.

- -

A wicked person flees when no one is chasing him, but righteous people are as bold as lions.
PROVERBS 28:1 GW

59

Delight God's Heart

Heavenly Father, I rejoice in my relationship with You. Today I offer the purest worship through thanksgiving. Thank You for the many undeserved blessings You bestow on me daily. You provide the air I breathe, the life I live, and the joy I experience. You hear my prayers always. I am grateful for Your presence; You are always near. I live my life today in absolute surrender to You. You have given me life, and I give my life back to You. I am filled with awe at the opportunity to do life together.

- - - - - - - - - - - - - - - - - -

Since we are receiving our rights to an unshakeable kingdom we should be extremely thankful and offer God the purest worship that delights his heart as we lay down our lives in absolute surrender, filled with awe.
HEBREWS 12:28 TPT

60

In the City of My God

My future is secure in You, God. Thank You for making me more than a conqueror. I can be an overcomer in this life because I belong to You. When I am weak, You make me strong. When I am tired, You give me rest. You have written Your name on my life. I am forever a citizen of Your city. I will live forever with You. Give me strength to stand firm.

"As for the one who conquers, I will make him a pillar in the temple of my God; he will be secure and will go out no more; and I will write my God's Name on him, and he will be a citizen in the city of my God—the New Jerusalem, coming down from heaven from my God; and he will have my new Name inscribed upon him."

REVELATION 3:12 TLB

61

My Advocate

Thank You, Father, for sending the Holy Spirit. He forever serves as my Advocate to defend and vindicate me. He will always stand between me and my accuser. The Holy Spirit leads and guides me in every area of my life. When He speaks, I will listen because He comforts me and teaches me all things. He directs my steps with peace and helps me make wise choices for my life. He is my inward witness to show me Your best for me. I set my heart on this promise. Help me to diligently listen to the leading of the Holy Spirit.

"But the Advocate, the Holy Spirit, whom the Father will send in my name, will teach you all things and will remind you of everything I have said to you."
JOHN 14:26 NIV

62

Listen to Understand

Heavenly Father, I have been guilty of listening for my opportunity to speak, rather than seeking to truly understand others. You have placed me in people's lives to be a blessing to them. Give me courage to be a help to others as they share with me in conversation. Give me wisdom about each conversation. May I be that person of deep understanding. Teach me to draw godly advice from Your Spirit within me. Help me pour Your life and Your wisdom onto those who share their lives with me. Help me listen to them and to You and respond in love and truth.

- -

A motive in the human heart is like deep water, and a person who has understanding draws it out.
PROVERBS 20:5 GW

63

Put Me Back Together

Sometimes life brings wonderful and amazing things from You. Other times I find myself in a battle that I'm losing. On the days I want to quit, I know I can't. I am reminded that no matter how painful the situation or how broken I am, I am committed to You. Even when I feel like I've lost myself, with pieces of my heart scattered all over the place, somehow You find me and put me back together with Your Word. Whisper Your truth to me. I will never forsake Your way! I adhere my heart tightly to Your sayings. Your constant love renews me with the strength I need.

I've committed myself and I'll never turn back from living by your righteous order. Everything's falling apart on me, GOD; put me together again with your Word.
PSALM 119:106–107 MSG

64

Be Still

Lord, You know it's hard for me to be still. I feel like I need to be doing something, but You have strongly encouraged me in Your Word to be still so that I might experience Your salvation. Help me rest in You. I open my heart and allow Your peace to comfort me. I will shut my mouth and listen as Your wisdom speaks to me. I stand in the quiet of Your presence and wait. Only You can defeat my enemies; only You can overcome the challenges I'm facing. I am calm and obedient to Your voice. I wait with Your patience. You are fighting for me. I will be still and allow You to do a mighty work on my behalf.

- -

"The Lord is fighting for you! So be still!"
Exodus 14:14 gw

65

Keep My Footsteps Steady

Your Word is perfect and Your principles are long-standing and proven over many lifetimes. You revive my soul with Your wise and trustworthy commands. They fill my heart with joy. My love for Your laws keeps my footsteps steady, and I am safe. Lord, help me discern my errors, and forgive my hidden faults. Keep me from willful sins so that they will not control my life. May the words of my mouth and the meditation of my heart be pleasing in Your sight. Thank You for steadying me in troubled times with the truth of Your Word.

- - - - - - - - - - - - - - - -

The law of the LORD is perfect, converting the soul; the testimony of the LORD is sure, making wise the simple; the statutes of the LORD are right, rejoicing the heart; the commandment of the LORD is pure, enlightening the eyes.
PSALM 19:7–8 NKJV

66

Better Together

Heavenly Father, today I pray for my church and the body of Christ. I pray for unity. You have called us to be the full expression of Your Son. It hurts my heart when those in the church display character that is unlike Christ. We are a community. We come together to worship You but also to live our lives in a way that pleases You. May we bless one another and work together to grow in faith, becoming all that You have called us to be. Help us love one another and serve one another, as well as our community.

God has put everything under the control of Christ. He has made Christ the head of everything for the good of the church. The church is Christ's body and completes him as he fills everything in every way.
EPHESIANS 1:22–23 GW

67

Pursue What Is True

Lord, I'm wilting away. I'm discouraged by the hurts and pains I've experienced. I'm struggling to stand firm. Revive me by Your Word, just as You promised You would. Bring those scriptures to my mind, that I may draw courage and vigor from You. I open my heart to Your wisdom. May I see through deception and have great discernment about the decisions I must make. Light up my way with Your truth. Don't let me make a mess of this. Help me choose what is right. Make Your way clear. Help me pursue only what is true.

- - - - - - - - - - - - - - - -

Help me turn my eyes away from illusions so that I pursue only that which is true; drench my soul with life as I walk in your paths.
PSALM 119:37 TPT

68

Turn Worries into Prayers

Lord, You said worrying doesn't help me. So I look to You. I trust You to do as You've promised. You will perfect everything that concerns me. I bring my worries to You today. I turn those worries into prayers. I will search Your Word and discover Your promises. I will stand firm, speaking Your Word in prayer. By faith I believe You will make a way when I don't see one. I don't have to know how You will resolve the issue, but I trust that You are at work on my behalf to bring Your very best outcome.

- -

"And which of you by worrying can add one cubit to his stature? If you then are not able to do the least, why are you anxious for the rest?"
LUKE 12:25–26 NKJV

69

Standing in the Gap

Lord, today I stand in the gap for a friend. I may not know all the details of her situation, but You do. You know the circumstances. You know the need. You know the pain. You know the condition of the heart of everyone affected. Bring peace and hope to this situation. Wrap Your arms around my friend. Show her Your mercy and Your love. Give her words of wisdom, courage, and strength for the days ahead. Bring about Your perfect resolution to this situation. Give me whatever I need to be a support to her. Bless her, Lord, in every way.

- -

"So I sought for a man among them who would make a wall, and stand in the gap before Me on behalf of the land, that I should not destroy it; but I found no one."
 EZEKIEL 22:30 NKJV

70

Secure and Safe

God, thank You for being my refuge, a shelter when I am afraid. Throughout Your Word You encourage me to "fear not" because You are with me. My days are in Your hands. I trade my fears for faith. I give up my worries and my doubts and choose to trust You. You are faithful. I choose to live in the shelter of Your love, always hidden in Your strength. In You I know I am safe and secure. Today, I rest in Your place of protection. I release all the fears in this life and embrace You by faith, believing You will keep me in all my ways.

- -

When you sit enthroned under the shadow of Shaddai, you are hidden in the strength of God Most High.
PSALM 91:1 TPT

71

Promise Keeper

Lord, You are always good. You always do good to and for me. I choose to believe every promise You've made. You are not a man; You cannot lie. Your Word is forever established. Once You commit to a thing, it is done. You never change Your mind. For that reason, I can count on You. You will always keep Your promises. I look back on our relationship and see all the times that You did exactly what You said. Even though people have failed me, I have to remember that You cannot. Thank You for Your goodness. I will not doubt. I believe in You.

- -

"You are blessed for believing that the Lord would keep his promise to you."
LUKE 1:45 GW

72

For the Bibleless

Thank You, Father, for the Bible. I can't imagine not having Your Holy Word. Yet there are people who don't have a Bible in their language. They can't read about You like I can. They deserve to have Your truth at their fingertips. They long to know You and hear Your words. Make a way for them to have Your Word, Lord. Bring people together; build translation teams. May all people groups hear You speak to them in their own language. I pray that more people come to know the need for everyone to have Your Word in a language they best understand.

- -

I inherited your book on living; it's mine forever—what a gift! And how happy it makes me! I concentrate on doing exactly what you say—I always have and always will.
PSALM 119:111–112 MSG

73

Miracle Maker

Lord, here I am again. My prayers today are not for myself but for those I know and love. My heart hurts for someone. She's asked for prayer, and I'm interceding for her. You know what she is facing; You know the miracle she needs. So, God, I'm trusting You to do what only You can do. You are the miracle maker. When no one else can, You can. Show up in this situation. Pour out Your goodness, Your mercy, and Your grace. Repair and restore. The works of Your hands are unlimited. Make a way, even though we cannot see it. Let her see Your marvelous wonders. I know nothing is impossible for You.

- -

"He performs wonders that cannot be fathomed, miracles that cannot be counted."

JOB 5:9 NIV

74

God's Word Alive in Me

As I study the Bible, I plant seeds of Your Word in my heart. I pray that Your truths grow up strong in me. Just like a tree grows strong planted by a river, I grow stronger each day with the water of Your Word. I will never fail, because Your Word lives in me and Your Word will never fail. When I gave my life to You, Lord, You started a good work in me, and I know that it will continue in me until You return.

- - - - - - - - - - - - - - - - - - - -

For this reason we also thank God without ceasing, because when you received the word of God which you heard from us, you welcomed it not as the word of men, but as it is in truth, the word of God, which also effectively works in you who believe.

1 THESSALONIANS 2:13 NKJV

75

Testimony of Goodness

My life is a testimony of Your goodness, Lord. May all who look at me see You. Let my life point others to You. You are a refuge when I am in trouble. You comfort me when I feel alone. You defend me from my enemies. You are my hope and my confidence. It's not what I can do but what You achieve through me. I am grateful for Your mercies. I give You praise for all the times You've rescued me, even the times I'm not aware of. Glory and praise to Your holy name!

- - - - - - - - - - - - - - - - -

Magnify the marvels of your mercy to all who seek you. Make your Pure One wonderful to me, like you do for all those who turn aside to hide themselves in you.
PSALM 17:7 TPT

76

God Always Hears

God, sometimes I'm tempted to believe the lie that You don't hear me when I pray. But You are with me always. You hear me every time I call on You. When Jesus prayed, He acknowledged that You heard Him, and so I acknowledge that You always hear me. Even if I don't sense a reply or feel I have the answers I need, I trust that You still hear me. The answer will come eventually. Thank You for listening. And help me wait patiently, listening to You.

And Jesus lifted up His eyes and said, "Father, I thank You that You have heard Me. And I know that You always hear Me, but because of the people who are standing by I said this, that they may believe that You sent Me."
JOHN 11:41–42 NKJV

77

So Much More

Lord, I'm learning that prayer is not just asking for things. It's not bringing You a list of wants and trying to tell You how I'd like it all worked out. It's truly spending time in Your presence, talking with You and listening for Your reply. Increase my desire to be close to You. I want to know You, experience You, and wait in Your presence. You are my source, truly the only one I can forever depend on. Talk to me. I open my heart. I'm listening. Tell me what I need to hear. I align my heart and my desires with Yours. More than anything, I want to be connected to You.

- - - - - - - - - - - - - - - - - - -

You ask and do not receive, because you ask amiss, that you may spend it on your pleasures.
JAMES 4:3 NKJV

78

By Grace

God, You knew me before I was born. You called my name and planned my way. I am nothing without You. It is by Your might and power that I am who I am. You reached down in Your great love and pulled me up. You planted me on a path You had for me. Nothing can take me out of Your hand. Your grace and mercy go before me. You have led me to the place I'm at today. You never remind me of my mistakes and misgivings. You see me through the eyes of love. You give me success. Thank You for all Your blessings. By Your grace, I am what I am.

- -

By the grace of God I am what I am.
1 Corinthians 15:10 niv

79

When God Surprises

Heavenly Father, You give the best surprises. It's taken me awhile, but I'm learning that when I ask You for something, You deliver beyond what I can ask or even imagine. Forgive me for the times I've been impatient and ungrateful. I'm sorry. I couldn't see what You were doing behind the scenes. I never should have doubted that You were at work. Your love never fails. Give me grace to wait for Your perfect surprise. Thank You for the sweet, unexpected things. Help me to never take the small things for granted. I trust You and love You with all that is in me.

- -

"Where is your faith?" he asked his disciples.
In fear and amazement they asked one
another, "Who is this? He commands even the
winds and the water, and they obey him."
LUKE 8:25 NIV

80

Pure Light

Jesus, You are the Light of the World. Nothing is hidden from You. You bring light into the dark corners of my life and cleanse me. You have saved me from the darkness; You have freed me with Your love. I have nothing to fear. Remove all deception from my heart. May I always run to You. Flood me with Your life. Shine a light that keeps me from stumbling. Guide my life by Your pure light, and let that light shine through me, bringing Your joy and life to others. Give me strength to help those around me break free from the darkness.

- - - - - - - - - - - - - - - -

Life came into being because of him, for his life is light for all humanity. And this Living Expression is the Light that bursts through gloom—the Light that darkness could not diminish!

John 1:4–5 TPT

81

My Place of Quiet Peace

This world is so loud; it constantly shouts for my attention. My head fills up with so much stuff—things I need to do, questions I need to answer, and never-ending activity. The fast-paced merry-go-round of life won't stop, but I can step off. Help me remember to take time to slow down, to sit down and become quiet with You. Nowhere else do I experience the peace You provide. I need time with You every day. Help me to diligently spend those quiet moments with You. Let Your peaceful presence wash over me and quiet my soul.

- -

You're my place of quiet retreat;
I wait for your Word to renew me.
PSALM 119:114 MSG

82

Breathe Prayers

You tell me in Your Word to remain in an atmosphere of prayer. You are always with me, and I want to be listening every moment. Please fill my heart and mind with a desire to stay in communication with You throughout my day. Tune my heart to hear You. May Your Spirit flow through me just like the air I breathe in and out. Let my thoughts be on the work You have for me to do. Fill me with compassion for others. May my lips be ready to speak Your truth in love to those around me, but give me wisdom to know when to be quiet and breathe out a prayer instead.

"The Spirit of God made me what I am,
the breath of God Almighty gave me life!"
JOB 33:4 MSG

83

Our God Will Fight for Us

Heavenly Father, I totally depend on You always—but especially in the battle. Help me remember that I have a part as well. I will do all that is necessary to prepare for battle. My final confidence is in You, but I will not neglect doing what You tell me in Your Word. I will stand firm in faith. I will take up the full armor of God so that when the day of battle comes, I am able to stand my ground. Then, having done everything I can, I will stand firm and watch You fight for me. You go before me. I am certain, with no doubt, that You will fight for me.

- - - - - - - - - - - - - - - - - - - -

"When you hear the trumpet, assemble around me. Our God will fight for us!"
NEHEMIAH 4:20 GW

84

Back Together Again

Lord, I've cried out to You in my troubles so many times, I've lost count. Thank You for always being there. No matter the number of times I fall apart, You always comfort me in the middle of grief, loss, sorrow, or failure. You are my promise, and I cling tightly to You. You hold me close and save me. Even though my tears blur my vision and I can't see where the pieces of my heart have been scattered, You pick up the fragments and put me back together again. You stand me up, strengthen me, and show me the truth of where I am, as only You can.

The Lord is close to the brokenhearted and saves those who are crushed in spirit.
PSALM 34:18 NIV

85

Compassion

Jesus, I want to be filled with Your compassion. You love me unconditionally. Forgive me for thinking less of other people. No matter who they are or how different they are from me, You love them. And for that reason, I should show them Your love. Forgive me for being judgmental. Give me eyes of compassion to see them as You do. Give me opportunities to demonstrate kindness. Show me ways to bless those I would normally avoid. Remind me to pray for and acknowledge others just as You would.

Since you have been chosen by God who has given you this new kind of life, and because of his deep love and concern for you, you should practice tenderhearted mercy and kindness to others. Don't worry about making a good impression on them, but be ready to suffer quietly and patiently.
COLOSSIANS 3:12 TLB

86

First Place

I give Your Word first place in my life. I walk in the light of Your Word, stepping where You shine the light of truth, trusting that I am always in the right place at the right time in order to live according to Your purposes. In everything I do, I desire to bring You honor. I want to please You. I refuse to veer to the right or the left of the path You've set before me. It comforts me knowing You are always with me. I listen as Your voice speaks to me, telling me the way to go.

- -

"So shall My word be that goes forth from My mouth; it shall not return to Me void, but it shall accomplish what I please, and it shall prosper in the thing for which I sent it."

ISAIAH 55:11 NKJV

87

Simply Follow

Forgive me, Lord, for making obedience harder than it is. I feel like I'm unprepared for what You've asked me to do, but really, I have a hard time letting go. Give me courage to step out, trusting You'll provide everything I need to accomplish the task. You will give me wisdom to act and the words to speak. You will equip me. All I have to do is follow You. I courageously declare that I will do what You've asked. I will step out in faith and trust You to meet me along the way.

The Spirit of the Sovereign Lord is on me, because the Lord has anointed me to proclaim good news to the poor. He has sent me to bind up the brokenhearted, to proclaim freedom for the captives and release from darkness for the prisoners.
ISAIAH 61:1 NIV

88

Miracle Words

Lord, how I love Your words—miracle words! Wonderful and true, they are life and healing. Looking back, I see how Your words sustained me. Looking forward, I know Your words will prepare a path before me. As I follow You in all You ask, I will surely find the destiny You have prepared. The opening of Your Word pours light into my soul and gives me supernatural understanding. I choose Your wisdom. I receive Your discernment. Speak to me in the nighttime so that I may rejoice with singing in the morning. I am forever thankful for Your words of life!

- - - - - - - - - - - - - - - - - -

Every word you give me is a miracle word—how could I help but obey? Break open your words, let the light shine out, let ordinary people see the meaning.
PSALM 119:129–130 MSG

89

Restoration and Provision

Lord, my job is not my source. You are my source. You always provide for me. When my workplace is difficult, You help me be a blessing to others. When my employer is unfair, You are my justice. And if I lose my job, You will restore me to wealth. I will never go hungry or beg for bread. My needs are never a surprise to You; You know what I need before I ask You. And yet, I ask because You've asked me to do so. You abundantly supply my every need. It may be uncomfortable at times, but I will live by faith. I will stand firm and believe the best is yet to come.

- - - - - - - - - - - - - - - - - - - -

*The LORD their God will take care of them
and will restore their fortunes.*
ZEPHANIAH 2:7 GW

90

My Keeper

Thank You, heavenly Father, for keeping me in all my ways. When I leave the house, I trust You to give me wisdom to navigate my day in safety so that I can return home without accident or incident. You give me strength when I am weary. You listen to my pleas for help as well as my praises. Your eyes are always on me, and Your ears are always listening for my voice. When I speak, You always hear me. You keep me steady. When I reach out to You, I find You. I can always depend on You. I am grateful for You, my keeper!

- -

He will guard and guide me, never letting me stumble or fall. God is my keeper; he will never forget nor ignore me.
PSALM 121:3 TPT

91

Satan, Take a Hike

God, when I said yes to You, I invited You to work Your will in my life. Purify my life. I am here, down on my knees before You. I am committed to Your ways. And I stand firm against the enemy. I refuse to give him any opportunity. With all of heaven behind me, I say to him, "Satan, take a hike. You no longer have any hold over me. I am a child of the Most High God!" God, You are in charge. You are closer than my breath. Lead and guide me all my days.

- - - - - - - - - - - - - - - - - -

So be subject to God. Resist the devil [stand firm against him], and he will flee from you. Come close to God and He will come close to you.

JAMES 4:7–8 AMPC

92

Your Word Makes Anything Possible

Heavenly Father, Your Word is limitless and unbreakable. Thank You, God, for giving me Your Word—Your promises for all eternity. You cannot lie. You say it, and it is so. I choose to trust and believe Your Word above all else. I will grow in faith and stand firm on You and the power of Your Word. It is alive and working in my life. I know that when I speak Your truths and apply faith, the Word will accomplish what You send it to do in my life. You will keep me in perfect peace as I build my life on Your Word. Thank You for making the seemingly impossible a reality in my life.

- - - - - - - - - - - - - - - - - -

But Jesus looked at them and said to them, "With men this is impossible, but with God all things are possible."
MATTHEW 19:26 NKJV

93

Dreams and Aspirations

Lord, I commit my aspirations to You. I believe that those dreams within my heart were placed there by You and that You have a plan to bring them to fruition. Give me the courage to work toward my goals and not be swayed by the opinions of others. Renew my mind and spirit so I'll be able to test and approve what Your will is—Your good, pleasing, and perfect will. Help me pace myself and learn the things I need to know before I put plans into motion. I will be humble and conscious of the hopes and hearts of others. I will praise You and give You all the glory as we work together for Your good.

- - - - - - - - - - - - - - - - - -

The aspirations of good people end in celebration; the ambitions of bad people crash.
PROVERBS 10:28 MSG

94

Guide Our Nation

Jesus, we are a hurting nation, an angry nation, a nation struggling to maintain our values while still dealing firmly with opposition. Guide our nation's leaders during these difficult times. We trust in You and long for Your guidance and peace. Give our leaders divine wisdom and heavenly revelation according to Your plans and purposes for our nation. Bring Your people together to unite in prayer and stand firm in faith for revival in our land. Bring salvation, comfort, and peace to our culture. Protect and keep us from our enemies. Shut the mouths of those who speak against You. May every person come to have a personal relationship with You.

- - - - - - - - - - - - - - - - - - -

Now therefore, O you kings,
act wisely; be instructed and warned,
O you rulers of the earth.
PSALM 2:10 AMPC

95

My Road, Revealed by God

Heavenly Father, I will stay true to You. You have placed me on the right path. Nothing can take me out of Your hand. I am confident in Your truth. You have plans for me, and those plans are good. You knew me before I was born, and You planned my way. You walk with me and talk with me. When I ask, You answer. When I look to the right or to the left, You whisper gently, "This is the way to go. Follow Me." I am focused. I will stay on course. I refuse to be deterred from walking the road You've chosen for me. Thank You that I don't ever have to walk alone.

- - - - - - - - - - - - - - - - -

You're blessed when you stay on course,
walking steadily on the road revealed by God.
PSALM 119:1 MSG

96

Navigating Decisions

Lord, I desire to please You more than anything else. Help me ask You the right questions in order to sense Your wisdom and realize the answers You have for me. Help me not to be afraid of the answers but to trust You. Please show me how You look at this situation. Give me eyes to see things from the right perspective. Help me learn and grow in my faith as I navigate this decision. Help me let go of any thoughts that are contrary to Your Word. I trust You will give me the answers I need so I understand clearly the next step to take.

- - - - - - - - - - - - - - - - - - - -

But let endurance and steadfastness and patience have full play and do a thorough work, so that you may be [people] perfectly and fully developed [with no defects], lacking in nothing.
JAMES 1:4 AMPC

97

Give Hope. Give Life.

Mighty God, You are my hope. You have given me life and delivered me from death. My faith is rising. I believe I will receive all that You have prepared for me. My life is Yours to command. I look to You for all the answers. When I don't yet see what You see, help my unbelief. Holy Spirit, please let me see what You see, and make me courageous enough to follow through with Your divine appointments—encounters that could change a life. I trust You. I know You are my reward. I earnestly seek to know You more.

- - - - - - - - - - - - - - - - - - - -

But without faith it is impossible to please and be satisfactory to Him. For whoever would come near to God must [necessarily] believe that God exists and that He is the rewarder of those who earnestly and diligently seek Him [out].
Hebrews 11:6 ampc

98

A Long Drink of Salvation

God, it's important to revive my spirit with Your presence. Your Word fuels me. Praise music and moments of worship recharge my spiritual batteries. When I'm tempted to disconnect and close myself off from You, remind me that my health—soul and body—comes from You. I invite You to interrupt my busy life and prompt me to spend time with You.

"If you'll hold on to me for dear life," says GOD, "I'll get you out of any trouble. I'll give you the best of care if you'll only get to know and trust me. Call me and I'll answer, be at your side in bad times; I'll rescue you, then throw you a party. I'll give you a long life, give you a long drink of salvation!"
PSALM 91:14–16 MSG

99

My Hope Rises

Jesus, Your words in the Bible encourage me. I speak Your Word with my mouth and hope rises in my heart. I will fight fear with faith knowing Your glory and truth will overcome the darkness. No darkness can withstand even a sliver of light. I choose to walk in Your light each day. Your gift of resurrection life pushes back the darkness. When I am tempted to allow the darkness to creep into my thoughts, remind me to shine Your light on those thoughts, knowing it will expel the darkness.

- -

Arise, shine; for your light has come! And the glory of the LORD is risen upon you. For behold, the darkness shall cover the earth, and deep darkness the people; but the LORD will arise over you, and His glory will be seen upon you.
ISAIAH 60:1–2 NKJV

100

You Do Miracles

Thank You for doing miracles in my heart and in my life. Forgive me when I've doubted, and help me trust You more each day. When You speak to me and give me a promise, I will hold fast to it. I will believe You and encourage myself in Your Word. Even when the miracle looks like the smallest thing—such as a cloud the size of a man's fist—I will stand strong and see the rain poured out lavishly on my life. Your Word says we all have a measure of faith given to us. I will use my faith today to believe that You will faithfully complete the work You've begun in me.

- -

You are the God who performs miracles.
You have made your strength
known among the nations.
PSALM 77:14 GW

101

Set for Life

God, my life is in You. You alone are my rest. I find peace in Your presence. Thank You for Your all-surpassing strength. When I stumble, You hold me up. I refuse to be shaken by the challenges facing me. When I can't catch my breath, You pour oxygen into my soul. I will not be moved when things don't go my way. I will rise above the disappointment because my future is assured. Because of You, I am set for life. In You, I have everything I need.

- - - - - - - - - - - - - - - - - -

God, the one and only—I'll wait as long as he says. Everything I hope for comes from him, so why not? He's solid rock under my feet, breathing room for my soul, an impregnable castle: I'm set for life.
PSALM 62:5–6 MSG

102

To Speak the Truth, Always

Lord, let the words of my mouth and the meditations of my heart be pleasing in Your sight. Your Word says that life and death are in the power of my tongue. I know what is in my heart comes out my mouth. Help me pause and think before I speak, especially in delicate or awkward situations. Create in me a clean heart. Holy Spirit, fill me with a new attitude and new motives. Quicken my heart to hear things the way You do. Tune my ear to hear what I'm saying. Help me speak with love and kindness.

- -

"Your very words will be used as evidence against you, and your words will declare you either innocent or guilty."
MATTHEW 12:37 TPT

103

Run to God!

Father, on hard days, help me not to grumble or fuss with You like a small child. Shut my mouth so I don't complain to others. I can be such a whiner! When I am angry, teach me to run *to* You instead of *away* from You. When I encounter difficulty or disappointment, remind me that I can never hide from You. When I feel scared, weak, or alone, hold me tight and don't let me go. Lift my heart and give me strength. Remind me of all You've done. Bring Your promises to life in me, and help me push through the hard places. I do love You with all my heart and soul. You are my strength in every circumstance—good or bad.

- -

The Lord is a strong fortress.
The godly run to him and are safe.
PROVERBS 18:10 TLB

104

Whispers of Encouragement

Lord, You've given me all the answers. They are found in Your Word. When I feel lost and far from You, please remind me of Your truth. Let Your words speak to me as though You were whispering encouragement and direction into my ear. Hold me up with the power of Your Word when I feel defeated. Give me strength when I feel drained by my circumstances. Direct my eyes to the scriptures You would have me read for the answers I need today. You know what I need before I even ask.

- - - - - - - - - - - - - - - - - - - -

"This Book of the Law shall not depart from your mouth, but you shall meditate in it day and night, that you may observe to do according to all that is written in it. For then you will make your way prosperous, and then you will have good success."

JOSHUA 1:8 NKJV

105

Right Words

God, I need Your help. I need a lot of courage for a difficult conversation I must have. I have to tell someone something that's tough to say. I need to be truthful, but it's so hard, God. Please give me the right words. Help me say things in a way that will help and not hurt. Please speak through me. Prepare her heart for what You would have me say. Give me Your grace to do what is necessary.

We should no longer be children, tossed to and fro and carried about with every wind of doctrine, by the trickery of men, in the cunning craftiness of deceitful plotting, but, speaking the truth in love, may grow up in all things into Him who is the head—Christ.
EPHESIANS 4:14–15 NKJV

106

To Answer the Call

Thank You, Lord, for knocking on the door of my heart. Thank You for giving me the courage to answer and invite You into my life. Now I ask You to help me encourage others to answer that same knock on their heart's door. Help me pay attention when You bring people across my path who are ready for a seed of hope to be planted in their hearts. Give me Your words to speak into their lives; guide me in actions that support them. May I respond with a heart of compassion and a disciplined life as an example to them.

--- --- --- --- --- --- --- --- --- --- ---

Behold, I stand at the door and knock; if anyone hears and listens to and heeds My voice and opens the door, I will come in to him and will eat with him, and he [will eat] with Me.
REVELATION 3:20 AMPC

107

Rescue Me

"Lord, listen to my prayer. It's like a sacrifice I bring to you; I must have more revelation of your word! Take my words to heart when I ask you, Lord; rescue me, just like you promised! I offer you my joyous praise for all that you've taught me. Your wonderful words will become my song of worship, for everything you've commanded is perfect and true. Place your hands of strength and favor upon me, for I've made my choice to follow your ways. I wait for your deliverance, O Lord, for your words thrill me like nothing else! Invigorate my life so that I can praise you even more, and may your truth be my strength!" (Psalm 119:169–175 TPT).

- -

I'll never forget what you've taught me, Lord,
but when I wander off and lose my way,
come after me, for I am your beloved!
PSALM 119:176 TPT

108

Holding on to Hope

Lord, I refuse to quit! I'm holding on to hope. My hope is in You, my Rock and my Redeemer. If I did quit, I realize I would just become stuck. The only way out is to put one foot in front of the other. Give me strength to endure this season. Eventually it will pass. I must keep pressing on day after day. I will come out of this on the other side. I will look back and see just how far we've come together. I wait with expectation, even if the end is not in sight. I won't let go. You are the answer. You are where I've placed my hope.

- - - - - - - - - - - - - - - - - - - -

Wait, Israel, for GOD. Wait with hope.
Hope now; hope always!
PSALM 131:3 MSG

109

Truth's Shining Light

Heavenly Father, thank You for the Bible. It is filled with everything I need to follow after You. Like a bright flashlight in the darkest of nights, it shows me the way forward toward the life You have for me. It guides me in wisdom, helping me see the stumbling blocks in my way so that I can navigate carefully over them without falling. When I am frustrated or confused, Your truth makes the way clear for me. When my heart is troubled about life's circumstances, Your words bring me back to a place of peace found only in You.

- - - - - - - - - - - - - - - -

Truth's shining light guides me in my choices and decisions; the revelation of your word makes my pathway clear.
PSALM 119:105 TPT

110

No Deceit

God, I messed up today. I deceived someone. Thank You for convicting me, not condemning me. Your love gently presses me forward to do what is good and right. I refuse to blame others or offer excuses. I take full responsibility for my actions and words. Please forgive me. Help me have the courage to tell the truth. Thank You for helping me choose the right words that will bring about reconciliation in this situation. Please lead me to examine my life and get rid of everything that doesn't draw me closer to You. Lead me now.

For let him who wants to enjoy life and see good days [good—whether apparent or not] keep his tongue free from evil and his lips from guile (treachery, deceit).
1 PETER 3:10 AMPC

111

Invitation to God

God, You're always invited to do life with me. I want to walk with You and experience all You have for me in this life. I study Your Word so that it abides in me, strengthening me in all things. May Your wisdom cry out to me, and may I always listen. I give You full access to my heart. Sweep out the old things and make Your home in me glorious and new. Speak to me, guide me, and direct me. Show me the way You want me to live.

Let the word of Christ live in you richly, flooding you with all wisdom. Apply the Scriptures as you teach and instruct one another with the Psalms, and with festive praises, and with prophetic songs given to you spontaneously by the Spirit, so sing to God with all your hearts!
COLOSSIANS 3:16 TPT

112

Appreciate the Moment

God, the world is moving so fast! I think about all the changes I've seen in my lifetime and it's amazing. Sometimes I just want to make time stand still. Today, I stand still and drink in Your peace. I recall the times of Your goodness. I look at the life You've given me, and I listen. I take in the minutes and seconds. I appreciate this moment in time. Help me not to lose sight of You in the blur of my days. I loosen my grip and let go of all of life's pressures. I relish this quiet time and relax in Your presence.

- - - - - - - - - - - - - - - - - - - -

Let be and be still, and know (recognize and understand) that I am God. I will be exalted among the nations! I will be exalted in the earth!
PSALM 46:10 AMPC

113

Power, Fall on Me

Father, I welcome Your presence. I need a great big drink of Your love. Come to me, as in the days of old. Shake me and wake me until I fully grasp Your power. Fill me with Your strength. Open my eyes to see more of You. Give me a freedom to flow in Your goodness—freedom like I've never experienced. Give me boldness to proclaim Your name. Fill me with courage to declare Your will in a mighty way. Pour out Your truth to all humankind. Use me as You will.

- -

And when they had prayed, the place in which they were assembled was shaken; and they were all filled with the Holy Spirit, and they continued to speak the Word of God with freedom and boldness and courage.

ACTS 4:31 AMPC

114

Placing Worry in His Hands

Father, strengthen my heart. Give me the courage I need to overcome fear. I know that You love me and watch over my family and friends far better than I can. I come to You with palms up and arms open wide. I release what I want to hold close. I give You the lives of those I love. I can't protect them or make their lives better. Help me put my worries about them in Your hands. You know their names. You love them more than I do. Give me peace as I let go of them today.

- - - - - - - - - - - - - - - - - -

*"Who will not fear you, Lord, and bring glory to your name? For you alone are holy.
All nations will come and worship before you, for your righteous acts have been revealed."*
REVELATION 15:4 NIV

115

Miracles Every Day

Lord, You are the miracle maker. Forgive me when I miss the small, everyday miracles. Help me see everything You are doing, all that You provide in my life. Teach me to be grateful for every gift You give. I will rejoice for every breath I take and every provision You make. I know You do great things. I believe You can bring the dead back to life. You make a way when there seems to be no way. You keep me from harm. I celebrate You, Lord! Thank You for being at work in my life even now, in this very moment.

- - - - - - - - - - - - - - - - - - - -

Jesus turned around and, seeing her,
He said, Take courage, daughter! Your
faith has made you well. And at once
the woman was restored to health.
MATTHEW 9:22 AMPC

116

Committed to the Journey

God, I want to continue to grow. Let my words, my thoughts, and my choices be pleasing to You. May all that I do be a witness to others. Sometimes it's hard to step out in faith because I don't know all the details. I must trust that You have a good reason for asking me to do this next thing. The secret to change in my life is to give all to You—to let go and let You work everything out for my good. Help me stay committed to the journey ahead, and remind me that others are watching.

- -

If I am being poured out as a drink offering on the sacrifice and service of your faith, I am glad and rejoice with you all. For the same reason you also be glad and rejoice with me.
PHILIPPIANS 2:17–18 NKJV

117

Fight My Battles

Father, You've told me who the enemy is. I'm not fighting with men and women. But we are fighting powers we cannot see. Remind me not to blame people when they are used by the enemy. I will keep my focus on You. You fight my battles for me. Give me a courageous heart so I can fight this fight with faith. I praise You in the middle of the battle. You have already declared me victorious. I am guaranteed a win—as long as I stand on Your side, the side of truth!

For we do not wrestle against flesh and blood, but against principalities, against powers, against the rulers of the darkness of this age, against spiritual hosts of wickedness in the heavenly places.
EPHESIANS 6:12 NKJV

118

Holy Spirit Power

Lord, today I pray for my family. As we go through this life, we each are tempted at times. I stand firm in faith that we will not falter. The Holy Spirit goes with my family, giving them the power to stand against any temptation. Holy Spirit, remind them who they are in Christ. Give them the Word of God to speak in the face of the enemy. May they always choose truth and life. Let them not be deceived in any way. May they hear the voice of Wisdom saying, "This is the way, walk in it." Infuse them with strength and power today.

Jesus, full of the Holy Spirit, left the Jordan River, being urged by the Spirit out into the barren wastelands of Judea, where Satan tempted him for forty days.
LUKE 4:1–2 TLB

119

Doubt My Doubt

God, I am filled with a sinking-like-Peter feeling right now. I felt courageous when my eyes were on You. But my circumstances began to roll like billows of the sea and began to overtake me. I looked down; I thought about the challenges. Buoy my faith, Lord, so I don't sink. As I meditate on how You control the wind and the waves, fill me with Your power, courage, and strength. I look to You. Gird me up, and carry me through the rough waters. Help me to doubt my doubt.

- -

But when he saw that the wind was boisterous, he was afraid; and beginning to sink he cried out, saying, "Lord, save me!" And immediately Jesus stretched out His hand and caught him, and said to him, "O you of little faith, why did you doubt?"
MATTHEW 14:30–31 NKJV

120

For Our Leaders

Lord, I continue to stand in faith and believe that You protect and keep our country. I pray today for the president and national leadership. May those who don't know You personally come to know You now. May You use our state and local leaders to bring prosperity and blessing to the people. Fill our church leaders with a compassion like Yours. May they teach Your truth in love; may they serve, inspire, and encourage us to love one another as You have loved us.

- -

I admonish and urge that petitions, prayers, intercessions, and thanksgivings be offered on behalf of all men, for kings and all who are in positions of authority or high responsibility, that [outwardly] we may pass a quiet and undisturbed life [and inwardly] a peaceable one in all godliness and reverence and seriousness in every way.
1 Timothy 2:1–2 ampc

121

No More Exaggeration

Sometimes I'm tempted to make things sound a little better than they are. It's easy to call it an exaggeration. That seems like less of a sin, but adding to the truth is a lie. I don't want to be a liar. Lord, confront me when I speak falsely, and help me to immediately say, "No, that's not true," correcting my mistake as soon as it escapes my mouth. Redeem me from this curse, Lord. Let my words always be truthful.

"You are of your father the devil, and the desires of your father you want to do. He was a murderer from the beginning, and does not stand in the truth, because there is no truth in him. When he speaks a lie, he speaks from his own resources, for he is a liar and the father of it."
JOHN 8:44 NKJV

122

Fear Can Never Conquer Me

God, Your Word says that You have given me a spirit of power, love, and a sound mind instead of fear. No matter how hard the season or how dark the night, fear has no place in my life. It will not conquer me, because You defeated fear for me. I stay close to You, always in Your presence. You are my strength and my peace. Your comfort surrounds me. Your perfect love casts away all fear.

- - - - - - - - - - - - - - - - - - - -

Lord, even when your path takes me through the valley of deepest darkness, fear will never conquer me, for you already have! You remain close to me and lead me through it all the way. Your authority is my strength and my peace. The comfort of your love takes away my fear. I'll never be lonely, for you are near.
PSALM 23:4 TPT

123

Stomp out the Doubt

When I am tempted to doubt the promises You've made, I will grow my expectations. I will dream big. I take my what-ifs and why-nots and I stomp them to the ground. Doubt and unbelief are not thoughts from You. Your Word says the devil is under my feet. So I place those thoughts that are against Your truth under my feet too. I remember Your Word. I will be brave and courageous. I will not give up. I will hold tightly to hope; hope is my anchor. I will endure. I will not be defeated. All of Your promises are yes and amen.

- -

Wait and hope for and expect the Lord; be brave and of good courage and let your heart be stout and enduring. Yes, wait for and hope for and expect the Lord.
PSALM 27:14 AMPC

124

Wise Counsel

Lord, I've been praying a long time about this situation, but it never seems to change. I'm asking You now, what should I do? Is it time for a different plan? Lead me to people who aren't afraid to speak truth into my life. Prepare their hearts to speak by Your Holy Spirit. Bring truth and wise counsel. Through their lives, their words, and their love for me, allow me to see what I might be missing. Once they've spoken Your truth, confirm it in Your Word. Let me know through scripture and revelation that You are leading me.

Where there is no [wise, intelligent] guidance, the people fall [and go off course like a ship without a helm], but in the abundance of [wise and godly] counselors there is victory.
PROVERBS 11:14 AMP

125

I Know You Love Me

I trust You, Lord. I am learning every day that no one else could ever love me like You do. I look at true human love in my life, and I realize Your love is beyond measure. No matter what comes my way, nothing can remove me from Your hand. Your unconditional, all-consuming love is powerful. It gives me the strength I need to step out in faith, to believe what others perceive as unbelievable. You counted me worthy of Your love, so I know I am precious and valuable.

- - - - - - - - - - - - - - -

For I am persuaded that neither death nor life, nor angels nor principalities nor powers, nor things present nor things to come, nor height nor depth, nor any other created thing, shall be able to separate us from the love of God which is in Christ Jesus our Lord.
ROMANS 8:38–39 NKJV

126

Be with My Children

Heavenly Father, thank You for the beautiful children You have given me to raise. I do my best each day to raise them in a way that pleases You. I pray that they know You, will love You more day by day, and will never turn from Your ways. Help me give them biblical wisdom. Show me what they need to become all that You desire them to be. Give me words when they need answers. Prepare my heart when it's time to let go, even if I'm just letting go a little. Comfort me as I remember that You are with them always.

By faith Moses, when he was born, was hidden three months by his parents, because they saw he was a beautiful child; and they were not afraid of the king's command.

HEBREWS 11:23 NKJV

127

On Mission

Sometimes people think that ministry is only for those who stand on the platform, but I am learning that ministry is face-to-face, one on one. Thank You for the missions You send me on each day. Thank You for those I love and the people You bring across my path. I want to be present in the moment with You, on mission to do what You desire of me. Whether it's a kind word, a moment of prayer, or something more, help me minister to others, just as You minister to me.

- -

"But I don't place any value on my own life. I want to finish the race I'm running. I want to carry out the mission I received from the Lord Jesus—the mission of testifying to the Good News of God's kindness."
Acts 20:24 GW

128

A New Thing

New seasons can be exciting, but they're not without challenges. I want to be excited about what You are going to do. I will not camp out on past failures or things I wish could have stayed the same. You have a purpose to every season. I am waiting and watching. I am expecting the new. I believe it will be a glorious surprise. I will not cower in trepidation but instead embrace it with joy. Give me an excitement for this new thing.

- -

Do not [earnestly] remember the former things; neither consider the things of old. Behold, I am doing a new thing! Now it springs forth; do you not perceive and know it and will you not give heed to it? I will even make a way in the wilderness and rivers in the desert.
ISAIAH 43:18–19 AMPC

129

Humility of Heart

I've worked hard, Lord. I've prayed, believed, and expected. I've imagined how You would promote me and bring blessing to my life. But I am learning that my way is not the way You will do it. Knocking down doors and placing myself above others, even if I think I deserve it, is not Your way. Forgive me for trying to make things happen. I want to do things the right way—Your way. I humble myself before You. I acknowledge that whatever happens for my good is not about me but about You at work *in* me. It is Your favor at work. Give me patience to wait for Your timing and the right promotion.

- - - - - - - - - - -

Humble yourselves in the Lord's presence.
Then he will give you a high position.
James 4:10 gw

130

Refuse to Quit

Lord, sometimes I want to say, "Beam me up, God!" I want to escape this place, with all its troubles and temptations. But You have given me life and definite purpose. I know You have work for me to do here. You know my passion. You created me with a uniqueness. I can do something no one else can do. I can touch lives perhaps no one else can touch for You. Let me help the hungry, the oppressed, the imprisoned, the homeless, and the wounded. Show me the plans You have for me. Give me strength for today. I refuse to quit! I will do all that You've asked me to do.

"But take courage, O Zerubbabel and Joshua and all the people; take courage and work, for I am with you, says the Lord Almighty."
HAGGAI 2:4 TLB

131

God Thoughts

God, sometimes negative thoughts consume me. I want to think Your thoughts for me, for my life, and for my future. I want to take my negative thoughts and turn them around so that they become positive, faith-filled affirmations. I will pay more attention to what I'm thinking. I choose to think on the truth, the reputable, honorable things. I need Your help keeping those negative, tempting, and worrisome thoughts under control. So I give You authority in my life to help me deal with my thoughts. Help me keep my mind on You.

Finally, brethren, whatever things are true, whatever things are noble, whatever things are just, whatever things are pure, whatever things are lovely, whatever things are of good report, if there is any virtue and if there is anything praiseworthy—meditate on these things.
Philippians 4:8 nkjv

132

A Place of Peace

Lord, You are my peace. I can't find peace in anyone or anything else. This world is full of chaos, and it does its best to crowd into my space. But You are my Rock, my confidence. I can step away from the race happening in this world. I can sit down in the quiet of Your presence and experience great peace—Your peace, not my own. Surround me even now, like a cloud, and go before me. Embrace me in Your peace that I may carry it with me and share it with others.

- - - - - - - - - - - - - - - -

Until at last the Spirit is poured down on us from heaven. Then once again enormous crops will come. Then justice will rule through all the land, and out of justice, peace. Quietness and confidence will reign forever more.
ISAIAH 32:15–17 TLB

133

Courage to Forgive

Jesus, You always forgive. You show compassion and are slow to anger. I know that's also the way I should be. When people hurt me, remind me to love like You do. Give me the courage to forgive even while they are doing what hurts me. As those who crucified You were nailing You to the cross, You prayed for the Father to forgive them. You had compassion, saying they didn't know what they were doing. Let my heart be filled with compassion for those who have hurt me or hurt someone I love. Let me truly let it go today. Fill my heart with understanding of just how much You love them. Let me see them like You do.

- - - - - - - - - - - - - - - - -

The soldiers, after they crucified him,
gambled over his clothing.
LUKE 23:34 TPT

134

Live an Authentic Life

It takes courage to live in Your light. It takes courage to remove the mask and live genuinely. I've watched the hypocrite and pretender. At times, I've even been one. But I am no longer a daughter of the dark; in Christ I am a child of the light. I can live with nothing to hide—no sin, no hypocrisy, no pretensions, nothing. I choose today to embrace the real me. I owe it to You, God, and to myself to live an authentic life.

- -

You groped your way through that murk once, but no longer. You're out in the open now. The bright light of Christ makes your way plain. So no more stumbling around. Get on with it! The good, the right, the true—these are the actions appropriate for daylight hours.
EPHESIANS 5:8–9 MSG

135

In Christ

God, You have rescued me from the power of darkness and brought me into the kingdom of Your Son. Jesus paid the ultimate price to free me, and my sins are forgiven. Because of His great sacrifice, I am no longer separated from You. I can walk into Your presence without sin, fault, or blame. And so, I accept the gift given to me. I put on the truth of who I am in Christ. I am grateful to You for giving me new life. I turn my face toward the new. Eternity is now—and forever with You. I choose to live in Your truth today.

- - - - - - - - - - - - - - - - - - - -

*He is the image of the invisible God,
the firstborn of all creation. . . .
He existed before everything and
holds everything together.*
COLOSSIANS 1:15, 17 GW

136

Spread God's Peace

Dear God, I pray for peace throughout the world, where there's so much pain, destruction, and disregard for Your creation. Some say peace is impossible—but with You all things are possible! Jesus declared peace for all Your children. We can never look to the world for true peace. That only comes from You. And although peace does not reign throughout the earth, it can reign in my heart. I can be a comfort to others in the middle of life's storms. Give me courage to speak life when things look dark. May Your peace be a tangible gift that I can share with others.

"Peace I leave with you, My peace I give to you; not as the world gives do I give to you. Let not your heart be troubled, neither let it be afraid."
JOHN 14:27 NKJV

Soul Rest

Most of the time I'm not very good at doing nothing. Even when I put my feet up, my mind races with thoughts of what I could or should be doing. I need calm inactivity. I know I don't make it a priority like I should. But today I accept Your invitation, God, to experience a deeper intimacy with You through times of rest. Each day I will courageously step back, look at what I'm doing, and give You the opportunity to search my heart. Remind me to do this. Please refresh me now.

- - - - - - - - - - - - -

When the Lord has given you rest from your sorrow and pain and from your trouble and unrest and from the hard service with which you were made to serve. . . . The whole earth is at rest and is quiet; they break forth into singing.
ISAIAH 14:3, 7 AMPC

138

You Make Up the Difference

Lord, I'm feeling a little deficient as a parent today. I want to be my very best for my family. When I'm not, it hurts my heart and I feel guilty, but I know that's not what You want for me. Forgive me, and help me forgive myself. Be at work in my children's lives. I trust You to make up the difference when I misstep. Your love covers all. Show me how to parent with Your love. Give me confidence in my decisions. I am doing all I can to be the parent my children need. I look to You for guidance. Help me discipline when necessary and show grace when that is best.

Most important of all, continue to show deep love for each other, for love makes up for many of your faults.
1 PETER 4:8 TLB

139

Morning Comes after the Storm

Father, You know the storms in my life, past and present. You know the one storm weighing heavily on my mind right now. The storm often feels stronger, more powerful, at night. My mind is flooded with negative thoughts, pouring in like ocean water that threatens to sink a ship. But You, my God, are my peace and my calm in the storm. I turn my face to You. I remember the times You took care of the storms of the past. Give me grace to navigate this storm as well. The morning will come and the storm will be no more. I rest in Your loving arms, safe and secure.

- -

Let the morning bring me word of your unfailing love, for I have put my trust in you.
PSALM 143:8 NIV

140

Increase and Wealth

Father, as Your child, I want to be able to give to every good work. I want to be successful in business and fruitful. You have given me the ability to produce wealth. Lord, bless my work and make everything I put my hand to become a blessing in my life and in others' lives. I study Your Word to learn Your ways. I lean into Your Holy Spirit and receive Your wisdom so that I make good and godly choices. Lead me in the way I should go. Show me the path You've set before me to bring honor and glory to You in my profession.

- - - - - - - - - - - - - - - - - - - -

But remember the LORD your God, for it is he who gives you the ability to produce wealth, and so confirms his covenant, which he swore to your ancestors, as it is today.
DEUTERONOMY 8:18 NIV

141

Shine the Light in My Community

There are dark forces at work in our schools, on our streets, and in our homes. I confront the enemy in the name of Jesus. Shine the light of Your glory and goodness into our community. Let Your light illuminate those who give way to evil. Let Your truth spring forth and eliminate the darkness. Protect and keep our first responders as they help us. Keep us safe from harm. You have overcome this world, Jesus. Give me the heart to intercede for others and the courage to protect the weak. Bring many of us believers together to stand against the darkness!

- - - - - - - - - - - - - - - - - - - -

The night is far spent, the day is at hand. Therefore let us cast off the works of darkness, and let us put on the armor of light.
ROMANS 13:12 NKJV

142

Rejoice! Rejoice! Rejoice!

I celebrate Your goodness! I cheer and exalt You. I exclaim Your integrity and praise Your holy name. I rejoice over the miracles You have done and the many times You kept me from destruction. I thank You for the great works You are doing even now, and I celebrate all that You have yet to do in my life and the lives of those I love. You have given me Your unfailing Word; it cannot return void. It always accomplishes all that You send it to do. I will speak Your Word of truth and be glad. I will see Your goodness in the land of the living. It will be manifested before my eyes.

Rejoice in the Lord always [delight, gladden yourselves in Him]; again I say, Rejoice!
PHILIPPIANS 4:4 AMPC

143

Powerful Encourager

Lord, I am grateful for the wonderful community You've given me. I can count on them to be there for me when I need support. What a blessing to have authentic people to do life with! They speak life and grace into my life. And they also give me opportunity to do the same for them. Help me be a powerful encourager for others. Bring people across my path who need to hear Your Word. Speak to them through me. Help me be open to receive Your truth and wisdom from those You've placed in my life.

And you must show mercy to those whose faith is wavering. Rescue others by snatching them from the flames of judgment. Show mercy to still others, but do so with great caution, hating the sins that contaminate their lives.
JUDE 22–23 NLT

144

God's Promise to Do Amazing Things

God, forgive me for my unbelief. Sometimes circumstances surround me and I am tempted to think You've forgotten me. But You would never abandon me. I remember the many times before when You rescued me. You showed up and delivered me. You've promised to do amazing things in my life. I am ready for a "suddenly"—a big surprise that will amaze me. I believe You will do abundantly above all I can ask or think. Help me wait with patience for Your timing. I praise You today, in advance, knowing something truly wonderful is on its way.

- - - - - - - - - - - - - - - - -

"Look at the nations and watch—and be utterly amazed. For I am going to do something in your days that you would not believe, even if you were told."
HABAKKUK 1:5 NIV

145

Hold on Tight

Lord, help me hold on tight to You. I don't want to miss a step, become deceived, or fall away. Let Your ways be made known to me. May they sink deeply into my understanding. It's not enough to hear Your desires for my life; I must focus my thoughts, my will, and my emotions in the right direction. Sometimes paying attention is hard work. I tune my spiritual ears to Your Word today. I will not just hear You but will also obey Your truths. I do not want to stray from Your plan. I desire to please You with all my heart.

This is why it is so crucial that we be all the more engaged and attentive to the truths that we have heard so that we do not drift off course.
HEBREWS 2:1 TPT

146

Make Known What Is Right

Lord, You have not kept my purpose hidden from me. When I seek You for what is right, You let me know Your ways and Your desires. You are the Lord, and You speak the truth; You make known what is right. You have given me Your true Word. You have revealed the secrets for Your will in my life. I don't have to search for evidence that what You've said will come to pass. I see Your plans at work through changes every day. Thank You for sharing Your Word and making what is right known to me today.

- - - - - - - - - - - - - - -

I haven't spoken privately or in some dark corner of the world. I didn't say to Jacob's descendants, "Search for me in vain!" I, the Lord, speak what is fair and say what is right.
ISAIAH 45:19 GW

147

A Godly Friend

Lord, I want to be a better friend. Help me be trustworthy and devoted. Help me put the desires of my friends before my own. Give me the power of encouragement so that I may be at their side. Cleanse me and give me a pure heart. May my purity of heart flow out in gracious and encouraging words. May Your wisdom and peace speak life and love into the hearts of my friends. Let my lips bring joy and peace. I trust You, Lord, to help my words and actions point all my friends toward knowing and loving You.

- -

He who loves purity and the pure in heart and who is gracious in speech—because of the grace of his lips will he have the king for his friend.
PROVERBS 22:11 AMPC

148

God's Decree

God, I refuse to give up! I've been waiting, pressing in, asking and trusting that everything You've promised will occur. Thank You for the joy and the strength You've given me to endure this season. Thank You for the small things that are bringing about Your purpose and plans. I agree with Your Word. All that You've promised is on its way. Even now, I believe blessings are flowing into my life. Your goodness will overtake me. I give You praise today for the overflow.

- - - - - - - - - - - - - - - -

"Things are going to happen so fast your head will swim, one thing fast on the heels of the other. You won't be able to keep up. Everything will be happening at once—and everywhere you look, blessings! Blessings like wine pouring off the mountains and hills."

AMOS 9:13 MSG

149

Perfecting Every Concern

Father, You know the weight I carry in my mind. You know all my thoughts. Help me rise above the thoughts that pervade my mind and influence my heart. Your mercy and love for me endure forever. They will never run out. You are at work in my life perfecting every single concern I have. You work all things out for my good. I turn my eyes to Your Word. I will put Your Word in my heart and trust You, that every word, every promise You have made will occur at the exact time You've purposed. I wait with patience.

The LORD will perfect that which concerns me; Your mercy, O LORD, endures forever; do not forsake the works of Your hands.

PSALM 138:8 NKJV

150

Shut the Liar's Mouth

Today I refuse to accept the lies the enemy of my soul is whispering to me. I am a child of the Most High God. I belong to You. Just as You reached down from heaven and rescued Daniel from the lions' mouths, I know You can shut the liar's mouth. I will stand firm in faith, trusting You for my deliverance. You kept Daniel safe overnight from the starving lions, and You have delivered me before. Give me strength to turn away from the lies, and fill my heart with Your truth.

"My God sent his angel and shut the lions' mouths so that they couldn't hurt me. He did this because he considered me innocent. Your Majesty, I haven't committed any crime."
DANIEL 6:22 GW

151

God-Aligned Decisions

God, I want to make all my decisions according to Your will. Your way is the right way. Above all, I want to follow where You lead in my life. I need Your wisdom today. I have a hard decision to make. It's difficult because there seems to be no solution that won't hurt someone. Help me find the path that You want me to go on—even if it's the rockiest one. Prepare the hearts of those I need to speak with so that what You give me to say is received in the best possible way. Give me courage, Lord.

- -

I will praise and give thanks to You with uprightness of heart when I learn [by sanctified experiences] Your righteous judgments [Your decisions against and punishments for particular lines of thought and conduct].
PSALM 119:7 AMPC

152

Take the Land

God, You have given me the land. Your goodness and mercy have provided all I need. You told the Israelites to possess the land, and I too will take possession of everything You've given me. All Your promises are mine. I will follow Your instructions. Speak to my heart. Lead me according to Your promises. Show me the path to take and the words to say. Go before me and prepare the way. I refuse to be afraid or become discouraged no matter the challenges because You have given me victory. I take possession by faith and hold on tight.

- - - - - - - - - - - - - - - - - -

"The Lord God has given us this land.
Go and possess it as he told us to. Don't
be afraid! Don't even doubt!"
DEUTERONOMY 1:21 TLB

153

His Spirit in Me!

Thank You, Jesus, for my salvation. I never have to worry about whether I am really a Christian. No one can ever convince me otherwise. The same Spirit that raised You from the dead resides in me. That power is available to me, and I lean into it. The Holy Spirit is working within me. He helps me with daily challenges and teaches me to pray. I am empowered to serve God and do His will. I am a part of God's plan on the earth. His Spirit operates and flows through me even now.

And if the Spirit of him who raised Jesus from the dead is living in you, he who raised Christ from the dead will also give life to your mortal bodies because of his Spirit who lives in you.
ROMANS 8:11 NIV

154

Love My Family

Thank You for the relationships You've placed in my life. Show me the purpose of each one. Family is important to You, so it should be important to me. Sometimes family relationships are hard because of history or difficult personalities. Give me wisdom to know how to navigate the difficult relationships. Help me flow in Your love even when my emotions don't want to cooperate. I want to be a blessing to my family and not a hindrance. Help me relate to them as You desire. Above all, let me love them in a way that would make them want to know You.

- - - - - - - - - - - - - - - - - - - -

Believe in the Lord Jesus Christ [give yourself up to Him, take yourself out of your own keeping and entrust yourself into His keeping] and you will be saved.
ACTS 16:31 AMPC

155

Let Others See You in Me

Heavenly Father, today I build myself up in my most holy faith, praying in the Spirit as You speak to my heart. Help me recognize Your truth and turn away from the enemy's attempts to deceive me. Give me a spirit of discernment. Give me words to say in every situation so that I may be a witness to others of Your goodness and love. Thank You for Your power and strength to embrace those things that grow my faith. Let others see You in me today.

- - - - - - - - - - - - - - - - - - - -

But you, dear friends, must build each other up in your most holy faith, pray in the power of the Holy Spirit, and await the mercy of our Lord Jesus Christ, who will bring you eternal life. In this way, you will keep yourselves safe in God's love.
JUDE 20–21 NLT

156

All Hope in Him

Today I place all my hope in You, God. I am learning that true peace can only come from You. I cannot depend on resting when a problem is resolved, because often more problems are just around the corner. It does me no good to worry, so forgive me when I do. Help me stand firm in my confidence, knowing *You* are my hope. I am strong and courageous when I rest in Your holy hand. You work all things together for my good. Because of Your unfailing love, all power and authority belong to You. You have the final say regarding everything that concerns me. I will not let go of You. You are where my hope comes from.

- -

"Power belongs to you, God, and with you, Lord, is unfailing love."
PSALM 62:11–12 NIV

157

Christlike Relationships

God, I am grateful to belong to You—to be Your child. Even more, I am thankful for my brothers and sisters in Christ that You have brought into my life. May I be a voice of encouragement to each of them. May Your words be my words when I speak into their lives as You inspire me to do so. May I speak with Your love, mercy, and grace. Give me ears to hear Your heart as You lead our conversations. May all my children—spiritual or natural—live according to Your truth. May we bring glory to You in our relationships.

- - - - - - - - - - - - - - - - - -

It is the greatest joy of my life to hear that my children are consistently living their lives in the ways of truth!
3 JOHN 4 TPT

158

The Day of Salvation

Father, waiting to live until my circumstances change is no way to live. I need to live now and enjoy the moments You've given me. I will live each day with thanksgiving and hope, knowing You are always at work; You are doing what is necessary to bring Your promises into my life at just the right time. *Now* is the right time to expect and experience Your saving grace, mercy, and love. You have answered me with a sure salvation. You have restored me and responded to me with an unbreakable promise.

For he says, I listened to you at the time of my favor. And the day when you needed salvation, I came to your aid. So can't you see? Now is the time to respond to his favor! Now is the day of salvation!

2 CORINTHIANS 6:2 TPT

159

Big-Picture Focus

Lord, each day that I have breath in my lungs is a gift from You. Forgive me for the times when my perspective has been on the problems I face. Help me make every minute count. Help me step back and enjoy the precious times You give me, with You and with those I love. Give me a big-picture focus. Let me look deeply at the things that really matter and gloss over those that don't. Reveal to me the things that I need to know by Your Spirit.

- - - - - - - - - - - - - - - - - - -

"Eye has not seen, nor ear heard, nor have entered into the heart of man the things which God has prepared for those who love Him." But God has revealed them to us through His Spirit. For the Spirit searches all things, yes, the deep things of God.
1 CORINTHIANS 2:9–10 NKJV

160

Living a God-Fashioned Life

You know I have struggled to put the past behind me. My old nature, before Christ, still tries to hold on to me. I no longer want that life. You have made me new. And I want, more than anything, to live my life fashioned after You. Thank You for seeing me as that new creature. I will become a person who accurately represents You. Give me courage to give up the excuses and get rid of what doesn't please You. Today, I take off the old and walk away.

That old way of life has to go. It's rotten through and through. Get rid of it! And then take on an entirely new way of life—a God-fashioned life, a life renewed from the inside and working itself into your conduct as God accurately reproduces his character in you.
EPHESIANS 4:22–24 MSG

161

I Trust You

So many things have happened in my life that I don't understand. I've been angry and frightened and wanted answers. But today I choose to trust You, Lord. With all my heart I choose to acknowledge You. You know what You're doing. My life is in Your hands. I don't have to know why. I want the details, but if You decide I don't need them, then I submit to You. I let go of it all. Courageously, I step out in faith, believing You are leading me toward the best outcome. You will show me the way to go, and I am determined to follow You.

Trust in the Lord with all your heart and
lean not on your own understanding;
in all your ways submit to him, and
he will make your paths straight.
PROVERBS 3:5–6 NIV

162

I Love You, Forever and Always

Lord, I love You. You shield and defend me from the seen and the unseen. When circumstances suddenly go a different direction than I thought, I trust that You have prevented a more terrible thing from coming into my life. When I think I have no more strength for the struggle at hand, You become my strength. You are my defender and my deliverer. You pull me out of the mess. You are my salvation. You continually save me from anything I need to be saved from. I rest in Your arms. No matter what comes, I love You forever and always.

- - - - - - - - - - - - - - - - - - - -

The Lord is my Rock, my Fortress, and my Deliverer; my God, my keen and firm Strength in Whom I will trust and take refuge, my Shield, and the Horn of my salvation, my High Tower.
PSALM 18:2 AMPC

163

No More in Darkness

Heavenly Father, I no longer live in fear of the darkness. Endless nighttimes are no longer my companion. I am grateful that I can now reside in the freedom of Your glorious light. Through Christ, You have opened the door for me to share in His inheritance. You have given me every spiritual blessing. You rescued me from the devil's dominion and adopted me as Your very own child. You planted me inside Your eternal kingdom, forgave all my sins, and redeemed me from any judgment. Thank You for all I have in Christ. He is the Truth, the Way, and the Light!

God has rescued us from the power of darkness and has brought us into the kingdom of his Son, whom he loves.
COLOSSIANS 1:13 GW

164

Going Forth, Stronger Than Before

Lord, I am standing in the middle of transition. Many things that used to be are no longer so. It's time for me to lead myself and others in a forward motion. Although my responsibilities are changing, I am not without help. You've provided the training and preparation. I have all I need. You have placed me on a firm foundation. I am ready to go forth, building on what I've learned, moving on stronger than before. When I am uncertain, remind me to look back at the experiences You've given me. I will draw wisdom from my journey so far.

- - - - - - - - - - - - - - - - - - - -

Hold tightly to the pattern of truth I taught you, especially concerning the faith and love Christ Jesus offers you.
2 TIMOTHY 1:13 TLB

165

Holy Invitation

God, You are a holy fire, roaring through the forest, consuming everything in Your way. You cannot be contained. I invite Your Holy Spirit to burn through me, devouring everything that is worthless and sinful. Create in me a pure heart and let only what is good and dedicated to You remain. I let go of the things that keep me imprisoned, like selfishness, insecurity, pride, and envy. You are filled with compassion. Your love saved me from sin and death. Give me a desire to see others set free. Ignite my heart, and fuel a passion in my soul to do the things You've asked me to do. Set things in motion today that will help me achieve the dream You've given me.

- - - - - - - - - -

For our God is a holy, devouring fire!
HEBREWS 12:29 TPT

166

Blessed Assurance

Heavenly Father, my salvation is a wonderful gift—something I could never earn, but a treasure given freely with no strings attached. It is mine and can never be taken from me. Nothing can separate me from Your love. Forgive me for the times that I doubted my salvation or thought it was something I needed to achieve or win. Thank You for believing in me, trusting me with Your love. I can stand in confidence each day knowing that I am saved and that I belong to You. My salvation is assured.

- - - - - - - - - - - - - - - -

And by this we know that we are of the truth, and shall assure our hearts before Him. For if our heart condemns us, God is greater than our heart, and knows all things. Beloved, if our heart does not condemn us, we have confidence toward God.
1 John 3:19–21 nkjv

167

Freed from Death

I take courage today knowing I belong to the one who raised Christ from the dead. All power and dominion belong to You. Because of Your willingness to give Your one and only Son, and His willingness to die for me, I have the opportunity to live my life in You. You have given me eternal life. I am forever restored to relationship with You. And eternity begins now. I don't have to wait for heaven; I have forever to spend with You. Death could not hold Jesus, and it cannot hold me. I have been freed from the grave.

"But God raised him from the dead, freeing him from the agony of death, because it was impossible for death to keep its hold on him."
ACTS 2:24 NIV

168

Astonishingly Blessed

Heavenly Father, You have poured, are pouring, and will continue to pour out Your power in my life in astonishing ways. I am always ready for anything and everything. Because You prepare me, I am more than ready to do what needs to be done. Whatever I need, I can count on You to go above and beyond. You give freely. Your right-living, right-giving ways never run out. Thank You for Your astonishing blessings in my life every day.

And God is able to make all grace (every favor and earthly blessing) come to you in abundance, so that you may always and under all circumstances and whatever the need be self-sufficient [possessing enough to require no aid or support and furnished in abundance for every good work and charitable donation].
2 Corinthians 9:8 ampc

169

His Favor, Always

Heavenly Father, because I am Your child, I am blessed. Pour out Your favor on me. Forgive me for the times You've prepared a blessing and I got in the way. Forgive me for trying to make things happen all by myself—in my timing instead of Yours. Give me ears to hear wisdom when You speak. I will listen to those You've placed in my life to mentor me. I choose to be pliable and moldable; I don't want to be stiff and inflexible to Your will. I choose Your way and not my own. My plans are big, but in no way do they compare to Yours. You saved me. May Your favor rest on me all the days of my life.

- - - - - - - - - - - - - - - - - -

*And Esther obtained favor in
the sight of all who saw her.*
ESTHER 2:15 NKJV

170

Life Everlasting

I get lost in the busyness of life sometimes—a lot of the time—and forget that I am not of this world. My future is eternal. Help me remember what is important. Things of this life fade away when compared to eternity with You. Remind me to build up my treasure in heaven; this world is just a place I'm passing through. I am most thankful for everlasting life. Give me opportunities to share this truth. Give me words to speak as You stir hearts to receive this gift. May my life lead others to You.

"For this is how much God loved the world— he gave his one and only, unique Son as a gift. So now everyone who believes in him will never perish but experience everlasting life."
JOHN 3:16 TPT

171

Always Listening

Lord, You are always with me. You are my audience of one. You never miss a single thing. I know for certain that You always hear me. Even when I feel alone and Your voice is difficult to hear because of the noise in this busy world, You are listening. Never let me believe the lie that You don't care. I love You and You love me. I trust that You are always working on my behalf. You have my best interest at heart. You bring all things together for my good in Your perfect time.

I am passionately in love with God because he listens to me. He hears my prayers and answers them.
PSALM 116:1 TPT

172

Listening to God's Direction

Father, thank You for Your wisdom. I've not always taken the time to ask You which way to go before moving forward, or even if I did ask, sometimes I didn't wait patiently for an answer. I desire Your will for my life. I want to be in the right place at the right time. May I move with You, forever listening for Your voice for direction. Show me the way I should go. Speak to me when I've gone off on my own. Bring me back to the place of peace—a place I can only find in You. Your ways are not my ways. Help me to always choose Your path for my life.

Whether you turn to the right or to the left, your ears will hear a voice behind you, saying, "This is the way; walk in it."
ISAIAH 30:21 NIV

173

Comfort during Loss

Jesus, You know my sorrow, my grief, my pain. No one truly understands my heart—but You. I have a lot of questions I want to know the answers to, and perhaps those answers can only come from You. Show me the path that is right, because sometimes I am blinded by my grief. Hold me tight as I let the tears fall. Wash away the brokenness. Help me let go of the pain and say goodbye to all the hurts. Fill me with Your peace.

- -

Blessed be the God and Father of our Lord Jesus Christ, the Father of mercies and God of all comfort, who comforts us in all our tribulation, that we may be able to comfort those who are in any trouble, with the comfort with which we ourselves are comforted by God.
2 Corinthians 1:3–4 nkjv

174

Follow Close to You

Lord, I live in a messed-up world. When bad things happen to good people, it's difficult for me to understand. I know that You hold my life in Your hands. My time is not my own, but Yours, and yet I desire a long life filled with Your goodness and love. Forgive me for the times I've closed off areas of my heart to You. I open them wide. When I call, You always answer. When I feel like I'm fighting a battle alone, give me assurance that You are with me. I will follow close to You. Hide me from my enemies, and keep me in safety next to You.

- - - - - - - - - - - - - - - - -

Yes, Lord, help us against our enemies, for man's help is useless. With God's help we shall do mighty things, for he will trample down our foes.
PSALM 60:11–12 TLB

175

Revive My Soul

God, I don't want to miss anything You have for me. I want to know You more. I want to go deeper in my relationship with You. Stir up Your life in me. Give me a desire for revitalization in my soul. Help me recognize distractions that keep me from reaching those goals You want me to reach. Show me how to speak life to others in a way that points them to You. Fill me with a passion for Your kingdom. Speak to me. Guide me. I want to be used for Your glory. May all I do bring You pleasure all the days of my life.

Revive us, and we will call upon Your name. Restore us, O LORD God of hosts; cause Your face to shine, and we shall be saved!
PSALM 80:18–19 NKJV

176

With Me through the Fire

Lord, You told us in Your Word to expect difficulty in this life. Your Word is full of miracles where You protected those You loved. I think of how You stood in the fire with Shadrach, Meshach, and Abednego. The fire was so hot that the people who threw them into it died, and yet they walked out without smelling like smoke. I cling tightly to Your promise today that when I go through the fire, I will not be burned up. The flames cannot consume me, because You are with me. I will emerge from this circumstance, and I won't even smell like smoke. Thank You, Lord!

When you walk through the fire of oppression, you will not be burned up— the flames will not consume you.

Isaiah 43:2 TLB

177

With Gratitude

You have been with me from the beginning, Lord. You have kept my foot from slipping and lifted me out of deep pits. You hold me up when the world falls away before me. You have hidden me from my enemies. You have saved the lives of my family. Forgive me for my complaints. I will never forget Your hand on my life. Thank You for the times You've turned things around and made a way when I could see no way. You have brought me this far, and with gratitude from deep in my heart, I thank You!

Then King David went in and sat before the Lord, and he said: "Who am I, Sovereign Lord, and what is my family, that you have brought me this far?"
2 Samuel 7:18 niv

178

To Honor the Lord in My Relationships

Lord, I pray for believers. I am part of the body of Christ. May we live in fellowship with You and with one another. May we come together in unity. Show me today how I can strengthen my connection with fellow believers and serve them. Help me use my gifts to build others up in faith. Give me words of wisdom and a heart of understanding to work with my brothers and sisters in Christ in a way that pleases You. Thank You for divine relationships. Thank You for those You've called to be a part of my life and my destiny. May I always honor You in my relationships.

Don't you realize that together you have become God's inner sanctuary and that the Spirit of God makes his permanent home in you?

1 CORINTHIANS 3:16 TPT

179

My Work Is a Joy

Lord, You have given me talents and gifts, and I desire to use them for Your glory. Thank You for giving me work to do and for blessing the work of my hands. Help me be diligent in whatever You put before me. May I work earnestly, with honor and integrity. Give me joy as I work because I do everything as unto You. Sometimes work is harder than I expected. Sometimes there are things that seem unfair. Help me remember that You've placed me exactly where You want me. Thank You for the opportunity to touch others with my life. May all I do bring them closer in relationship with You.

Whatever your hand finds to do,
do it with all your might.
ECCLESIASTES 9:10 NIV

180

Undeniable Love

Father, You are love personified. Everything You do is out of love. You loved me so much You gave Your one and only Son as a sacrifice so I could have a relationship with You. Thank You for choosing to love me unconditionally. May the undeniable love You've shown me be evident in my life. Let the Holy Spirit empower me to show Your love. Help me see love as a choice and not an emotional response. I desire to live my life poured out for others, demonstrating Your love to them in every word and deed.

By this the love of God was displayed in us, in that God has sent His [One and] only begotten Son [the One who is truly unique, the only One of His kind] into the world so that we might live through Him.

1 John 4:9 AMP

Scripture Index

OLD TESTAMENT

Exodus
14:13 3
14:14 64
33:11 32

Deuteronomy
1:21 152
31:6 24
8:18 140

Joshua
1:8 .... 27, 104

2 Samuel
7:18 177

Nehemiah
4:20 83

Esther
2:15...................... 169

Job
5:9 .... 54, 73
33:4 82

Psalms
1:1 25
2:10 94
17:7 75
18:2 162
19:7–8 65
23:4.......................122

27:3.........................7
27:7–8 48
27:14......................123
34:18 84
40:1–2 4
46:10 112
60:11–12 174
62:5–6..................101
62:11–12 156
77:14....................100
80:18–19...............175
91:1 70
91:14–16 98
94:19 1
116:1 171
119:1 95
119:7 151
119:10–11............55
119:37 67
119:40 33
119:105.................109
119:106–107...........63
119:111–112.........72
119:114 81
119:129–130 88
119:176 107
121:1–2...................34
121:3 90
131:3 108

138:8 149
139:16 39
143:8 139

Proverbs
3:5–6 161
4:20–22 40
10:28 93
11:14 124
12:25 30
17:22 19
18:10 103
20:5 62
22:11 147
28:1 58

Ecclesiastes
3:11 ....2, 38
9:10 179

Isaiah
14:3, 7 137
30:21 172
32:15–17 132
41:13 13
43:2 ....15, 176
43:18–19 128
45:19 146
49:16 14
54:13 53
55:11 86
60:1–2 99

61:1 87

Jeremiah
29:11 51
30:17 45
33:6 42

Ezekiel
22:30 69

Daniel
1:8 23
6:22 150
9:23 12

Amos
9:13 148

Habakkuk
1:5 144

Zephaniah
2:7 89

Haggai
2:4 130

NEW TESTAMENT

Matthew
9:22 115
12:37 102
14:30–31 119
19:26 92
22:31–32 26
24:35 56

Mark

6:50–51 8
9:23–24 22
9:36–37 28

Luke

1:45 71
4:1–2 118
7:9 29
8:25 79
11:1 46
12:25–26 68
23:34 133

John

1:4–5 80
3:16 170
8:44 121
10:10 44
10:27–28 5
11:41–42 76
14:26 61
14:27 136
16:22 49

Acts

2:24 167
4:31 113
9:17 36
16:31 154
20:24 127
27:25 31
28:30–31 10

Romans

5:8 43
8:11 153
8:28 18
8:34 6
8:38–39 125
13:12 141

1 Corinthians

2:9–10 159
3:16 178
10:13 9
15:10 78
16:13 52

2 Corinthians

1:3–4 173
5:17 35
6:2 158
9:7 17
9:8 168

Ephesians

1:22–23 66
4:14–15 105
4:22–24 160
5:8–9 134
5:13–14 21
6:12 117

Philippians

2:17–18 116
4:4 142

4:6 11
4:8 131

Colossians
1:13 163
1:15, 17 135
2:6–7 50
3:12 85
3:16 111

1 Thessalonians
2:13 74
5:16–18 57

2 Thessalonians
2:16–17 .... 16, 37

1 Timothy
2:1–2 120

2 Timothy
1:13 164

Hebrews
2:1 145
3:6 .... 41, 47
11:6 97
11:23 126
12:28 59
12:29 165

James
1:2–3 20
1:4 96
4:3 77

4:7–8 91
4:10 129

1 Peter
3:10 110
4:8 138

1 John
3:19–21 166
4:9 180

3 John
4 157

Jude
20–21 155
22–23 143

Revelation
3:12 60
3:20 106
15:4 114

Grow Deeper in Your Faith!

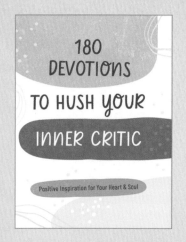

These 180 "glass half full" devotions and inspiring prayers will reassure your doubting heart. In each encouraging reading, you will encounter the bountiful love and grace of your Creator, while coming to understand His plan—for you and you alone. *180 Devotions to Hush Your Inner Critic* is a wonderful quiet-time devotional guaranteed to help you see yourself—and your place in the world—in a more positive light!

Hardback / 978-1-63609-725-1